Praise for Jorge Cruise
and *The 3 Choices*

*"Resilience, happiness, and freedom come from
knowing the choices that you have in front of you. This is
a remarkable, philosophical, and practical book that gives
you the power to start living your life to the fullest."*

— Don Miguel Ruiz, internationally best-selling author of
The Four Agreements and Toltec master, www.miguelruiz.com

"Sets you up to win!"

— Anthony Robbins, entrepreneur and #1 *New York Times*
best-selling author of *Unshakeable*

*"Jorge Cruise's advice on self-acceptance
and deep breathing has changed lives
and can change yours too."*

— *OK! Magazine*

*"Jorge Cruise takes a three-pronged
approach to overall health."*

— *Harper's BAZAAR*

*"Jorge Cruise's Jedi mind tricks
set you up to win."*

— *Redbook* magazine

the **3**
CHOICES

ALSO BY JORGE CRUISE

jorge cruise

the**3**

CHOICES

Simple Practices
to Transform Pain
into Power

HAY HOUSE, INC.
Carlsbad, California · New York City
London · Sydney · Johannesburg
Vancouver · New Delhi

Cataloging-in-Publication Data is on file
with the Library of Congress

ISBN: 978-1-4019-4606-7

10 9 8 7 6 5 4 3 2 1
1st edition, June 2017

Printed in the United States of America

To my husband, Sam.
Thank you for bringing the calm to my Latin fire
and for helping me see my hidden power.

CONTENTS

WELCOME LETTER

Dear Friends,

Over the past 20 years, I've had the opportunity to change the lives of millions of people as a health coach and best-selling author. I've shared a lot of important information throughout my career, but the greatest lessons of all came from my own life. Although I'm no spiritual guru, I am a person who has gone through (and grown through) tremendous adversity.

Eight years ago, my life was unraveling. I discovered that I was living the life I'd always wanted—but not the life I'd always *needed*. It was this detour (which you'll read more about in this book) that taught me that **life doesn't just happen; it is sculpted by the choices that we make**.

Now, when I say *choices*, I don't mean the choice to be happy or the choice to move on. I'm talking about the everyday choices that can be camouflaged by the chaos of life. Think about it: how many choices do you have in front of you right now? You could stop reading this page and order a pizza, watch the news, unfriend your ex on Facebook, etc. Choices are infinite possibilities that surround us constantly.

What you are about to learn are **simple hidden choices that instantly empower you and get you back on track to where you need to be**. No matter what pain you have experienced in your life, this book will help you transform that pain into power. How do I know this? Well, I have had both peaks and valleys in my life, and I was guided out of those valleys to the path that I am on today by the three choices you'll discover in this book. These are the same choices that led me to discover my own authentic self and true destiny.

The three choices will help unlock your inner power, and the stories and activities in this book will help make the lessons stick. The power behind these three choices is that as you continue to make them and commit to them, there will be no detour you can't find your way out of. You will develop tools that guide you to the next right choice and the destination in life that you were meant for.

But before you begin, I want you to know that there is no such thing as a "wrong" choice. It's easy to let ourselves get thrown by a choice or a circumstance that feels like a failure. What you must remember is that your life is bigger than any specific choice or experience because you learn as much from the wrong choices as you do from the "right" ones. So get ready to learn and evolve from the choices that surround you.

The following pages will arm you with three choices that will change your life. All you have to do is start choosing them. Once you begin to make each choice, you will start to grow and understand what makes you, you. And when that epiphany happens in this book, you will discover that the path that you are looking for has been there all along.

With Peace & Purpose,

Jorge Cruise

HOW TO BEGIN
Break Your Illusions

"Have no fear of perfection—you'll never reach it."

—Salvador Dali

You.

Are.

Not.

Perfect.

In fact, *nobody* is perfect. I don't care if you are the Queen of England or George Washington himself. We are all human, which means that we are full of mistakes, flaws, and imperfections. And that's okay. Those mistakes are what make us who we are. We are not robots.

It's important to come to terms with the fact that we don't need to be perfect beings before we can start living in ways that make us happy.

So say it with me: "I am human."

Say it again, write it down, sing it, frame it, repeat it, Snapchat it.

Now that we have discovered that we are all *imperfectly* human, it's time to identify . . . **what's holding you back from the life you *really* want?**

Think about it for a moment. (Seriously . . . Don't read another line until you really pause and think about *what* you want most and what you think is holding you back from it.)

1

Having now asked everyone from my son Owen to former president Bill Clinton himself this question, I've found that answers typically involve some sort of obstacle or personal flaw: Lack of opportunity. Little confidence. A difficult childhood that continues to stay with us in our adulthood. Setbacks that seem impossible to heal from. The fact that you haven't met "the one." Not enough money to do what you want. All of the above.

All of these are understandably difficult hurdles to overcome. I've experienced many of them myself. However, with the wisdom I've gained from my own personal experiences as well as from working with thousands of clients over the years, I've come to realize that these obstacles aren't what's really holding you back.

So, what is?

Perfect illusions.

We live in a world now where we are judged against perfection. Think about it. We wake up every day chasing a perfect illusion set upon us by society. From Barbie to Beyoncé, Sheryl Sandberg to June Cleaver, we have placed such high standards on ourselves as humans that we forget that we aren't robots.

We make mistakes. We fall down. But what's important is that we get back up. It's okay to have a bad day. It's okay to break the rules. **It's more than okay, it's expected.**

Because guess what? We are human. (Okay, I'll stop repeating myself now.)

So whatever is holding you back is not your own personal failings, but instead your striving for the "perfect life" that society says we're all supposed to have. But there is good news.

You Have the Power

You can have the life you've always wanted. It's possible. Believe me, I found mine.

But it's not I who is in control of your destiny. I'm just here to show the path that led me to my happy life in the hopes of inspiring you to find yours. You have the power to give yourself the freedom to create the life you desire—and it lies within *three simple choices*.

I've found that life is made up of choices. Choices that we make consciously and subconsciously all the time. Think about it. You've chosen to buy or borrow this book. You are choosing to read right now. You are even choosing to breathe right now, yet you're not consciously aware of it. Simple choices are made moment by moment, by you and only you. That means that every choice you make can be a choice to live a happy life—and that's what the three choices will help you do.

You don't need years of therapy. Not a near-death experience. Not winning the lottery. Not traveling all around the world. Just three easy choices. As you continue to choose to read with me, you'll discover exactly what these choices are and how to effectively and easily put them to work in your life with results that will have you thinking, *OMG. How did I achieve that?*

Welcome to the beginning of your new life of total freedom from what is holding you back from what you want! Now, let's get started with a question. Take a breath and get ready to look within.

Is What You Want What You *Really* Want?

Have you ever had the experience of getting something you want, only to have it fall short of your expectations? Perhaps you received a birthday present you had been yearning for, but now you find the reality of it mediocre. Maybe you've even gotten *everything* you thought you wanted, but you're still feeling a sense that there's something missing.

Here's a flashback to my 2009. I had just released my book *The Belly Fat Cure* and was in New York City to promote it by filming a segment on *The View* with Whoopi Goldberg and Sherri Shepherd. Filming went amazingly, and the results people were experiencing from this book were incredible. I had hit another home run in the publishing world, and it would soon become a number one *New York Times* bestseller. Yet, as I made my way back to JFK International

Airport to fly home to my wife and children, I remember just feeling incredibly numb inside. The feeling lingered the whole flight back to California, and I was incredibly confused. I couldn't understand why I was feeling unhappy, sad, and empty.

I was a self-proclaimed perfectionist, and, from the outside, I had successfully created a "perfect life" for myself. I had the career I always wanted (check), I had earned celebrity status as a fitness and health trainer (check), and I was a *New York Times* best-selling author (check). I had married someone I considered my best friend (check), and I was the father of two beautiful boys (check). I had the big house (check), new cars (check), and all the gadgets and toys I wanted (check). But inside I felt empty. I felt lost. I felt like I had gotten everything I wanted, but still wasn't happy.

Here's the deal . . . I was living a life that wasn't authentic to myself. Outside was as perfect as it could be, but inside I was completely numb. I was working 12- to 14-hour days, my marriage had become more of a work partnership than a love relationship, and I was an absent father. Despite the big Latin smile I wore for the world, I felt like a robot just going through the motions of life.

When we start to have some kind of awakening, the first thing we tend to do is deny it and try to stop it any way we can. It's as if the awakening process throws up a big red stop sign, saying, "Turn away; you aren't ready to deal with all these emotions." But let's face it: working through painful emotions isn't exactly a day trip to Disneyland. In the back of our minds, we know that once we face the reality, the dominos will be set in motion, and there's no going back. We'll be forced to make changes—uncomfortable, even painful ones. The people around us will be impacted and potentially hurt. It's so much easier (not to mention totally human) to want to stay safe in that little cocoon we already know and call home.

And so I squelched all the emptiness, ignored all the issues, and tried even harder to be perfect. But running away is a race you'll never win. The emptiness I felt only grew more intense, until it was impossible to ignore. The truth was I had everything I thought I'd ever wanted—but it was not what I really wanted.

Did I want a picture-perfect family, a successful company, and many best-selling books? You bet.

But what I wanted even more than all that was to *feel good on the inside.*

I desperately wanted to wake up each day *feeling* joyful, fulfilled, and free to be myself. I remember watching a Folgers coffee commercial one day and being struck by how happy this man was every morning to wake up with his family and drink the perfect cup of joe. I thought to myself, *Why can't I wake up happy, like* that *guy? What's wrong with* me? (Of course, "that guy" in the commercial is just a paid actor pretending to be happy, but I chose to ignore that fact.)

Don't get me wrong . . . I wasn't expecting to live in a constant state of nirvana. Of course I expected life to have its ups and downs. But I knew that there had to be more than this. We didn't come into this world to spend time feeling dead inside. We're alive, so aren't we supposed to *feel* alive on a consistent basis?

As a celebrity trainer, motivation and transformation are my forte. So why couldn't I feel alive?

What Do You Really Want to *Feel?*

The more I looked around, the more I noticed how many of us, even after achieving what we thought we wanted, weren't consistently *feeling* the way we wanted. I had helped thousands of my clients lose weight, shed fat, and get in the best shape of their lives. This was something they'd all desperately wanted to do, something they'd thought would totally transform their lives. But once they'd gotten used to their rock-solid bodies, they still felt a nagging sense of emptiness.

My client Lauren seemed to have it all—the guy of her dreams, the perfect engagement ring, and the dream job—but she still felt something was missing. So Lauren decided to enlist me as her trainer to get healthy for her upcoming wedding and new married life. Three months later, she was stronger, healthier, and fitter than ever. Still, even though Lauren was changing on the outside, I could tell that there was a mental block preventing her from feeling empowered on the inside.

Lauren revealed to me that she'd lost her younger brother to cancer and her father had drowned in front of her on a family vacation. To cope with these traumatic experiences from her childhood, Lauren would turn to food to comfort herself. I realized that it wasn't enough to treat the external symptoms of an internal trauma. After all, I could give her all the knowledge she needed to create the perfect body she thought she wanted, but that wouldn't give her the feelings inside that she really wanted.

Many of us (myself included) have turned to food as a coping mechanism to deal with boredom, grief, and other difficult emotions and situations. But it's important to consciously understand that the habit of eating to feel better is one we must break. The comfort we get from eating is merely an illusion. It is like putting a bandage on a flat tire: helpful for a little while, but the gash is still opened and exposed.

When you have some sort of trauma, you must acknowledge it, take care of it, protect it, and heal it. You can't ignore its existence or pretend that it doesn't cause pain. You have to break the false illusion that you have created, the one that says that this other thing will help you achieve a perfect life. It starts with acknowledging your wound's existence to begin the healing process.

That is exactly what Lauren did. She realized that she was looking to the wrong things to give herself the feelings that she wanted. With help from her mother, her fiancé, and the three choices within this book, Lauren was able to find peace with the death of her brother and father and break free from the illusion that the pain wasn't there, and then heal herself by making peace with her past.

When it comes down to it, we're all on a quest to feel certain feelings. All we really want is to feel good inside and out. Yes, we want to reach our goals: we want to get married, climb a mountain, succeed in a career, get in shape, and so on. Those all matter. But, ultimately, it's not the goal itself that we're truly striving for. *We're looking to build lives that will allow us to feel more of what we want to feel.* Happiness, fulfillment, freedom to be ourselves, peace, love . . . That's what we *really* want.

The problem is most of us are so caught up in our day-to-day lives, so busy with our pursuit of perfection, that we aren't even sure how we feel *now*, never mind how we *want* to feel. So, before we go any further, let's get you crystal clear on what you *really* want.

When it all comes down to it, how do you want to feel? Your immediate response is probably "happy," which is great! But I want you to dive even deeper and identify what other emotions you want to experience. I've found that we often feel more excited and have much more clarity when we get *even more descriptive.* (I'm an author, so I have a love for adjectives and details.) Sometimes the word *happy* is thrown around so much, it loses its power and true meaning. I want you to get clear on what *you* want to feel right now. Yes, you want to feel happy, but what feelings include that for you?

One of the most powerful ways to discover these feelings is to use an emotion wheel. I discovered this tool many years ago when I was on a mission to become better in touch with my emotions after my mother passed away. I've used it on a weekly basis ever since to help me understand my feelings.

There are several different versions of emotion wheels, but all are basically visual representations of several major emotions based on distinct categories. The primary emotions are in the center of the wheel, and as you move outward, you move into more detailed categories that more accurately describe how you truly feel. Psychologist Robert Plutchik, who was the first to create a wheel of emotions, defined eight primary emotions: joy, trust, fear, surprise, sadness, anticipation, anger, and disgust.

TRY THIS: Explore Your Feelings with an Emotion Wheel

The emotion wheel is a powerful tool to determine what you really want to feel. The following is one created by Geoffrey Roberts to aid in his work as a life coach and pastor. The wheel is divided into seven primary emotions—happy, sad, disgusted, angry, fearful, bad, and surprised—and dozens of secondary and tertiary emotions.

First, look over the wheel and choose the three emotions you've experienced the most over the last six months. Go with what jumps out at you. There are no right or wrong answers here. Write those emotions down on a piece of paper or in a journal.

Next, choose the three emotions you *want* to be experiencing most of the time. Scan the wheel for the words that really light you up and make you feel most alive. Pretend you had a magic wand like Harry Potter and could wake up feeling a certain way each day; how would you want to feel? Circle the words on the page or write them down. (Special note: If words come to you that aren't on this wheel, just write them down. The crucial element is that you choose words that make you feel *alive*.)

There you have it. The answer to what you *really* want is those three feelings.

Compare the emotions you selected in the first part of this exercise with those in the second part. Is there any overlap? Can you imagine if you felt those latter emotions *every day*? The three choices you're about to learn in this book will give you the freedom to live into these feelings.

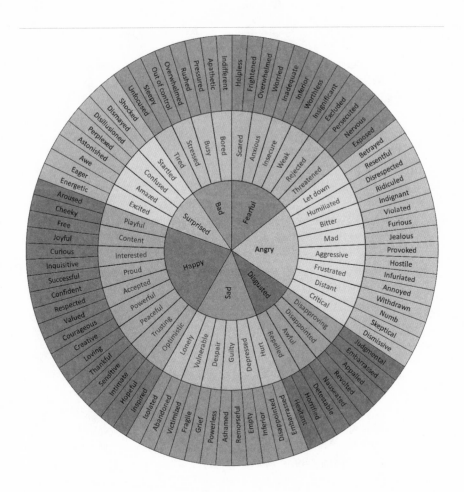

Let Freedom Ring

Over the years, I began my own quest to find out how to create a day-to-day life that would allow me to feel more of the feelings I wanted to feel. (Confession: I still envisioned a life like that Folgers coffee guy!) After a lot of soul-searching, a whole lot of crying, and some deep thinking, I realized that much of my current reality was the result of one thing: my choices.

Moment by moment, day by day, I had consistently been making choices out of fear and a need for approval. I was striving for the "perfect life" that society told me I wanted. Sure, at the time I thought I was making the right choices, but more often than not my choices were leading me to the very feelings I didn't want to have: remorse, overwhelm, and embarrassment.

As I searched for the answers, I came to understand that it was my own choices that would allow me to create a life that brought me more of those feelings that I wanted to feel. As I continued to work on myself, I was able to hone my ideas into the three simple choices that you're about to discover for yourself.

Now, I know what you're thinking: *How can just three choices change my life and set me free? Is this guy for real? This sounds like one of those late-night infomercials I see on TV!* Well, a smart woman by the name of Oprah Winfrey once told me, "Life should be simple." When I stopped focusing on the deep details of my life, I was able to change the way I felt and start living again. As I started to make these three choices more often, my life began to change from the inside out. I suddenly felt like myself again.

And as I began to share these choices with clients, I watched them experience the very same results. I now wake up nearly every day feeling fulfilled, hopeful, loving, and most important, free. Everything that had been holding me back has melted away. My life is now very different from how it was seven years ago. It's exactly what I *really* want—as if it were custom-made just for me.

Does this sound really easy? Perhaps too good to be true? If you're scoffing and thinking, *No way will this work*—I get it. Trust me, the changes that have taken place in my life didn't happen overnight. It's not as if I made these three simple choices and—kaboom—sailed off into an eternal paradise, free of problems and suffering. This is not a quick-fix method. *The truth is there is no quick fix.* (Sadly, that is one thing Apple has not invented.)

As millions of us do, I spent many years trying and failing to find fulfillment. During my journey, I went to therapy, worked with a life coach, and read thousands of self-help books. As a leader in the health and fitness industry, I was lucky to often find myself on TV shows and at events alongside some of the greatest transformational teachers of our time. Every time I bumped into someone I admired, I'd interview him or her to get their firsthand experience (I love hearing people's stories and learning how they have evolved their lives over time). Their wisdom helped pave the way to where I am today, and within this book I will be sharing the powerful lessons I've had the luxury of learning from my mentors. But here's the deal: all this self-help was not the be-all-end-all answer. Once I had all the knowledge, I still had to take action from within. *Ultimately, I had to make the choice to change.*

Now, for the record, I still think the field of self-help contains many valuable tools as part of a process of discovery and healing. Most methods, including medication, hypnosis, and others, have their merits. The problem for many of us is that, as much as we know that following a program long-term will have great payoffs, sticking to those plans day after day, week after week, is another issue entirely. We, as humans, still need to *choose* to act.

Did you know that up to 60 percent of therapy clients do not return after their first session? The average dropout rates over the course of any type of therapy is about 50 percent. I believe that part of the reason that people have trouble sticking to a program is discouragement. Based on my own personal journey as well as my experiences working with hundreds of thousands of clients, I know that what best motivates people (myself included) are behavioral choices that begin to work the *instant* you practice them.

Why the Three Choices Work

Many of the techniques described in this book are based on teachings and practices from some of the greatest traditions and influencers of our time. The reasoning behind the methodology of each of the three choices draws from a long history and wide knowledge base. I'm simply distilling the essence of the deeps truths that have personally helped me and offering you the tools and guidance so that you too can easily and immediately implement them into your life.

The benefits of the three choices that you're about to learn have been proven by scientific research, which you'll read about in the upcoming chapters. These behavioral choices utilize specific actions to provide *immediate* results. When you feel their effectiveness as soon as you do them, it triggers your motivation to *keep* doing them. These three choices keep on working as long as you keep making them on a regular basis—and since they keep providing results, you keep feeling motivated. Furthermore, these choices produce a domino effect of long-term results that build upon one another. The more you make these choices, the more your reality starts to change into the life you *really* want.

After you've internalized the three choices, you'll also be better able to cope with stress. When it comes to stress, what you need to know is that your body is constantly seeking balance, or *homeostasis*. However, what keeps you in balance and what keeps me in balance will be a different set of nutrients, behaviors, activities, mindsets, and so on. It's important to discover what leads to homeostasis for you, and the three choices will help you figure this out.

One term that you'll often hear from researchers is *allostatic load*, or *allostasis*. This refers to being at the maximum carrying capacity of stress for you, including physical, mental, emotional, and so on. Your allostatic load is the "wear and tear" on your body in response to stress, which grows over time and from exposure to repeated or chronic stress. Keeping your allostatic load from becoming dangerous to your health means practicing the three choices to a happy life that you'll learn about in this book.

Each of these choices lightens your allostatic load by:

- Reducing stress in general

- Increasing your adaptation time so you can adjust to stress

- Shutting down stress when it happens, or keeping it from becoming overwhelming

That's what makes this method so unique. These are simple and effortless choices that provide powerful and effective results that transform your life, but again, let me be clear: this is no superficial fad. What you are going to learn is straightforward and fast working, but it is also highly motivating, and so it keeps you coming back for more (kind of like Ben & Jerry's ice cream, only this is much healthier). These three simple choices create big and complex changes that will lead to a metamorphosis in you as grand as that of a caterpillar to a butterfly. So get ready to spread your wings: it's your time.

Walk the Talk

I want to set you up for success, so there are a few recommendations I'd like to make so that you can fully reap the benefits from this book.

First, I recommend that you read this book in a short time span, ideally in less than a week. This is the absolute best way for you to take hold of the material so that the choices start to become second nature, as typical a part of your day as brushing your teeth is. I then suggest that you commit to making each of these choices at least once a day. Remember, they're simple, and you'll get immediate results. When you do all three on a consistent basis, you naturally begin to build the life that you truly want.

Each of the chapters of this book focuses on a different choice: "Be Imperfectly You," "Don't Hold Your Breath," and "Move to Improve." Each chapter is broken up into sections that focus on a different aspect of the choice, as well as lessons and teachings I've learned and benefited from throughout my time on this earth. The exercises in each chapter will help you practice and deepen your commitment to each choice. Then, at the end of each chapter, I offer a prescription titled "Your Rx," which is a schedule to help you internalize the lessons and incorporate them into your daily life.

One special note: The three choices are a process. Don't concern yourself so much with the end goal, but instead, work with the choices to the best of your abilities at that particular moment. Sometimes you might forget to make one of the Choices, sometimes you might mess up, sometimes you might even do the opposite. That's all okay.

Remember that you are human. What matters is that you stay with it and keep going. You will inevitably fall down, but you should *never* refuse to get back up. You deserve the life you really want, so don't ever think anything less of yourself.

One Last Thing . . .

Ultimately, everything you're about to read in the coming pages is just a reminder of the immense power you have within you. No matter what has happened in your past, no matter how you feel right now, no matter what others say, *you* are the master designer of your life. This book isn't in your hands by chance. Something within you wanted to break free, to feel more alive, to create a more extraordinary life.

You already made the simple choice to pick up this book. (Thank you for giving me the immense honor of helping you!) Now it's just a matter of making only three more easy choices . . .

Oh, and one extra one: first, you have to choose to turn the page. (See? It's already so easy!)

CHOICE 1
Be Imperfectly You

"You yourself, as much as anybody in the entire universe, deserve your love and affection."

— B u d d h a

The first choice you must make to free yourself from whatever is holding you back is to be who you are at your core—not who you think you should be or who others want you to be. Just be yourself. Be that person your soul talks to all day long. Listen to your inner self and just be you. Not who society wants you to be, not who your family wishes you to be, not even who your friends would like you to be.

Be imperfectly you. Because anything other than your imperfect self is not real. It's not who you are. Choosing to be your imperfect self is the most powerful choice you can make; it builds the foundation for not only the other two choices that change everything but also every single decision you make. Every time you make the choice to be imperfectly you, you will feel more empowered. And when you make this choice on a consistent basis, your entire life shifts toward a path more aligned with who you are at your core. You will experience more of the positive feelings you want and find the freedom to create what you truly desire.

Just be yourself. It seems like such a natural thing to do. After all, you've been getting to know yourself since you were born. So why does it *seem* so damn hard?

The truth is, it doesn't have to be. Seriously. Being yourself is something you are *supposed* to do. Hiding your true self doesn't help you or anyone around you.

By the end of this chapter, you'll manifest your imperfect self and have the tools to make this choice every single day. To get from here to there, I'll cover the three main aspects of being imperfectly you.

- *Understand and reconnect with your authentic self.* Here you'll gain a greater understanding and acceptance of your authentic self—that is, who you are at your core, the real you that exists without external pressure. You'll come to accept your core self and realize the importance of just being you and how that can positively change everything around you.

- *Accept your flaws.* In order to be your best self, you must embrace what you might be rejecting about yourself and your life. In this section, you'll learn how to rise above your perceived flaws and past difficulties.

- *Reveal and live the best you.* This is where the magic starts to happen. I'll teach you a simple, life-altering method that will enable you to access the best part of you, your most powerful core identity, and choose to live it every single day!

- *Your Rx: Everyday being.* In this section, I'll show you how to easily embrace your imperfect, authentic self in your everyday life.

So what's stopping you from making the choice to be imperfectly you?

Understand and Reconnect with Your Authentic Self

"To love oneself is the beginning of a lifelong romance."
—Oscar Wilde

From an early age, we're conditioned to live up to others' expectations, to march to the beat of someone else's drum, to long for approval. We're led to believe that it's more important to be liked and accepted than to be who we truly are. Think about it: There's a reason why there's a "popular kids" clique at every school. We are consistently searching for approval and acceptance from those around us.

Many of us are also given the false belief that we aren't good enough and therefore set out on a mission to fix ourselves. Unless you've become aware of who you are and have made a conscious choice to be just that, you're going to live a life that just never feels quite right. As a result, what you really want above all else—all those positive emotions you identified in the previous chapter—will be achieved in the short-term, at best, when you can instead wake up feeling them every single day.

Let me illustrate this with a story I've never told before about a little boy named George.

The Authentic George

On his tenth birthday, George finally received the gift he'd been wanting for years. Like every other energetic young boy on his birthday, George took no time to read the card and instead threw himself into quickly tearing off the wrapping paper, as if it were Christmas morning. George thought to himself, *Nooo, it couldn't be—how did she know?*

It was the Strawberry Shortcake doll he'd been wishing for every time he tagged along with his mom on a shopping trip. At first George was so happy that his mom's friend Mrs. Bowley knew what he liked. He quickly opened the box to play with his new strawberry-scented best friend, then paused. He looked up to see his Colombian grandmother, his mother's mother, frowning down upon him as if he had eaten dessert before dinner.

George suddenly remembered: He wasn't supposed to play with dolls. He wasn't supposed to do anything that girls did. George was to remain traditional and uniformed with all the other boys his age. Sadly, that doll was thrown away a day later by George's extremely traditional Catholic grandmother, and he never saw it again.

From the beginning of time, George's grandmother had one mantra, which was repeated to him over and over and over: "*Tu no eres maricón.*" In English, this translates to: "You're not a faggot." For the next 39 years, this mantra was gospel to George. Any time he had the slightest desire to be his true self, he heard his grandmother's reminder. This reminder prevented George from being George.

Throughout George's life, he always looked up to straight men as role models. He thought he just wanted to be like the men he admired. George wanted the six-pack, the muscles, the perfect smile, the gorgeous wife, and the big house. And guess what? George got everything he wanted. However, George was unaware that his subconscious appreciation for men held more of an intimate, rather than platonic, admiration. For the next 39 years George blocked his subconscious appreciation and focused on what he had been told his whole life: "*Tu no eres maricón.*"

One morning, while George was researching ways to train clients internationally, he stumbled upon a gay website. He suddenly saw gay men together, and he quickly panicked; he knew he couldn't be gay, but also couldn't quite understand his admiration for the men in front of him. When his wife entered the room, George showed her the different sites he had been researching. He didn't think anything of showing her the gay site he was on. There was no harm in researching it, and if George knew anything, he knew he was not gay. After all, this had been his affirmation since birth.

Still, the emotions that George felt after stumbling upon the gay site made him wonder if maybe there was something else he was struggling with. So George did what he does best, and researched the issue. He stumbled upon the book *Absent Fathers, Lost Sons*, written by Guy Corneau. The book described George's conflicted feelings and stated that the only reason why he was feeling this way was because his father hadn't been involved in his childhood. Feeling like he finally understood what had been wrong with him his entire life, George traveled across the country to seek professional help from a well-known therapist in New York City.

The therapist reassured him, "Of course you're not gay!" He then went on to explain that George's innocent interest in men was really because of his confusing childhood relationship with his father. In order to provide for his family, George's father had constantly traveled for work and was only able to see George on the weekends. The therapist told George to go back to the hotel he was staying at and visualize his father hugging him and saying, "I love you, son." George had never heard the words "I love you" from his father, so this exercise seemed very euphoric and freeing to him.

When George performed the exercise, he immediately started to hysterically cry. He thought to himself, *Wow, this is actually working.* So George sat and cried for hours as he visualized his father saying, "I love you, son." After four emotionally exhausting hours, George climbed into bed and slumbered so soundly that even Sleepy, the dwarf from *Snow White*, would be jealous. The next day, George woke up feeling invincible. He thought he was finally "cured" of all the feelings and emotions he had been having.

Relieved, George went back to his day-to-day life. But something was *still* off. He felt a pervasive sense of sadness. For years he kept working at his marriage, but it was becoming crystal clear that while he and his wife had a perfect partnership in business, their partnership at home had lost its magic. They agreed to a trial separation, and George sadly moved out of his "dream house."

A few days after the move, one of George's outspoken gay employees said what many people were probably already thinking: "Congrats on moving out, but when are you going to *come* out?"

George immediately became defensive. "What? No, I'm *not* gay," he replied. How could one of his own employees say this to him? Questioning his sexuality was a hard pill for George to swallow. Still, he invited his employee into his office to finish their conversation.

As the employee elaborated on what it meant to be gay, George was awestruck. He didn't believe *he* could be gay. After all why would someone "decide" to be gay? Why would someone want to go down a path where they are mocked and treated as a minority? The employee explained to George that being gay isn't a choice that you make, it's a facet of who you are at your core.

The employee offered to send research and articles to support this conclusion. Being a research-driven man himself, George accepted the offer and went home and read everything he could about being gay. He was stunned to find scientific research that proved that homosexuality is something that you're born with, just like the color of your eyes. It's part of what makes you you. Yet from the moment George had entered the world, he had been so strongly conditioned on who and what he was *supposed* to be, he never considered who he truly *was* deep down.

My Choice

The truth is, I, Jorge Cruise, am George.

And I am a gay Latin man.

I legally changed my name to Jorge in my midtwenties, as a way to honor my Latin heritage and pay homage to my mother after she had passed. (She always called me Jorge.) The name just felt more *me* as I started the process of owning who I truly was. But being gay? The truth is I had completely blocked out *this* part of my identity until that employee's outspoken remark hit me.

The funny thing is, since coming out, I've learned that so many people suspected that I might be gay. And my mom's friend who gave me that Strawberry Shortcake? I'm sure she knew I didn't just like the doll because I love strawberries. My grandmother definitely sensed I was gay from an early age, but worked hard (and quite successfully, I might add!) to get me to deny that part of myself to the point where I felt I had no choice.

But I *did* have a choice. I could choose to embrace who I was at my core, even if it wasn't exactly what I or anyone else wanted.

You also have a choice.

We're making that choice every day. I shared this very personal story to illustrate how deeply we can be conditioned into accepting or denying an aspect of our identity. But this one choice impacts all levels of our lives, from what you wear to your religion. For example, you choose to deny your core self when you:

- Choose a career that doesn't resonate with your soul.

- Harp on past mistakes instead of embracing your humanness.

- Don't speak up, voice your opinion, or share your feelings.

- Base your self-worth on the qualities that others deem important.

- Ask for advice more than you listen to your inner voice.

- Take on the labels others have given to you, such as "too sensitive" or "too lazy."

- Stop wearing things that you like because someone told you they were "too revealing" or "unflattering."

- Beat yourself up for perceived flaws.

- Put up a wall with others instead of letting them in.

The reality is that living authentically and being true to your core self isn't something to be taken lightly. In fact, it's a major cornerstone of mental health. According to the findings of the National Institute of Mental Health and National Science Foundation studies by Michael Kernis, a social psychology researcher at the University of Georgia, high levels of authenticity are linked to many aspects of health and well-being, including energy, self-worth, and life skills. On the other hand, low authenticity is linked to defensiveness, hostility, low self-esteem, depression, and anxiety. So it's important to be authentic and honest with yourself. As has been eloquently stated by so many (including Lady Gaga!), you were born this way, baby.

Own It

Being imperfectly you is about consistently choosing to be and live authentically. Every day, you decide to be yourself, show up as the best you, say what you mean, and do what resonates with you. You own all of who you are, including the parts of yourself that you aren't the biggest fan of. You endeavor to be your greatest self, but you never let that self-improvement get in the way of loving yourself as you are right now.

The more you make this choice, the more you will experience the following in your life:

- Fit comfortably inside your own skin, knowing that you belong in the life you are living, feeling truly free to live the life you choose.

- Naturally experience joy and passion on a daily basis.

- Know you are deserving of love, acceptance, money, joy . . . anything and everything you've ever wanted.

- Live the life you would freely choose if you knew you couldn't possibly fail.

- Be more able to connect with others and feel less lonely.

- Listen to that still, small voice deep inside that is always there telling you to be yourself—and then, be it, freely and fully!

- Appreciate what you have instead of complaining about what you don't.

- Open your eyes each morning, flooded with all the positive feelings you want, from happiness to enthusiasm and everything in between.

The real you is who you were created to be and are meant to be. It is the you who isn't influenced and defined by external pressure, by conditioning, by shoulds, or even by wants. It is you at your most authentic—genuine, unabashedly free, and pure. The real you isn't your job, your role, or your title. It consists of all the awesome skills, funny quirks, special talents, beautiful imperfections, amazing traits, and deep wisdom that are uniquely yours. When you are the real you, you feel most alive and free.

So how do you take off the masks and show up as the real you? The key is self-awareness. It's that easy, I promise.

Know Thyself

My morning isn't complete without a few essentials. A hug from my boys, a kiss from my husband, a double shot of espresso, a journaling session to get everything out of my head and onto paper, and a scroll through Facebook. (Let's face it. In today's world, social media is the new morning newspaper.) One morning, as I was browsing through my news feed, the following posts came up: a picture of my adorable niece, several news stories, and a personality quiz: "What Flavor of Ice Cream Are You?" Now, if you've read any of my other books, you know I'm not a proponent of eating processed sugar, but I was amused and intrigued. After I answered the silly questions, up came my real identity . . . strawberry ice cream! (I guess I really do have a thing for strawberries after all.)

Now, I'm telling you this story to make you laugh more than anything. If only it were this easy. One Facebook quiz, and ta-da: you know yourself inside and out! You're strawberry ice cream—now go out there and conquer the world! Of course, these fun quizzes aren't based on science (at least, not the ones I've seen). But it's always fascinating to me to see how many of my friends have taken them and what their answers are. And who knows, they may offer a little nugget of self-awareness.

The truth is, getting to know yourself is a lifelong adventure. Every day offers chances for new learning experiences and more self-understanding. There is no quick answer or final destination. However, with the following methods, you can learn more about yourself and deepen your connection with who you truly are. Remember, the more self-knowledge you have, the better you're able to choose to be imperfectly you.

The following activities worked for me personally as well as many of my clients, friends, and family. Feel free to try only the ones that resonate with you—or try all of them!

TRY THIS: Keep a Journal

Writing things down is perhaps one of the best ways to tap into your authentic self. Many years ago, the motivational speaker Anthony Robbins told me that if your life is worth living, it is worth recording. So every day, for the last 20 years, I've taken what's inside my head and put it down on paper. Okay, not actually paper. Like most others in our modern world, I'm usually scribbling away on my iPad!

My point is that when you spend time writing, away from the noise of the outside world, you're much more able to clarify your thoughts and feelings and gain understanding about yourself and life. Several studies have also shown that regular journaling lowers anxiety, reduces stress, improves sleep, increases IQ, and even improves your immune system.

So give it a try: I promise it will work. All you need to do is put pen to paper (or finger to screen) and start writing whatever comes to mind. Talk about the feelings and experiences you had today. If you're still not sure how to get started, consider using some of these prompts on a regular basis:

- One thing I know for sure right now is _____.
- The last thing I want to talk about is _____.
- I secretly desire _____.
- One thing I may be denying is _____.

TRY THIS: Take a "Me" Inventory

Okay, it's list time! (If you've decided to start keeping a journal, you can write the answers to this activity in there.) To be self-aware, you need to have a sense of the basics of your "self." I know this may seem daunting, but it's time to get familiar and open up that can of worms called "me." Ask yourself:

- What are my strengths?

- What are my weaknesses?

- What are my values?

- What do I love to do?

- What are my favorite books, movies, foods, places in the world, etc.?

- What makes me smile most?

- What makes me cry?

- What makes me excited?

- What makes me disappointed?

- What holds me back from expressing my true self?

- What makes me different from my family and friends?

- What makes me similar to my family and friends?

TRY THIS: Consult Your Tribe

Now, it may seem odd to ask others about who you are. After all, I'm telling you to be yourself and not look to others to tell you who you should be. Yet, sometimes, the people around us can see aspects of our true selves that we fail to notice. (Remember my outspoken employee telling me I was gay?)

This is particularly the case with our positive attributes. So many of us get caught up focusing on what we do wrong and where need to improve that we fail to see some of our greatest characteristics. So I recommend you select a handful of self-aware, positive people you respect (this is key) and ask them the following questions:

- What are three adjectives you'd use to describe me?

- What do you admire most about me?

- What is one thing you think I am great at?

My client Alex recently did this and was beyond shocked by how beautiful, confident, and witty people found her. While she saw herself as good-looking, she felt that she wasn't as attractive as her friends or husband. Alex's low self-esteem was paired with a lack of confidence in herself. She was sure that others would see her as negatively as she did! However, when she did this exercise, she was stunned to hear that many people found her attractive, outgoing, and intelligent. This consultation with her tribe helped boost her self-worth and allowed her to stop being so hard on herself. For the first time, Alex was able to see herself in the same light as everyone else did.

So give it a shot. You may be surprised to find that others find you just as confident and inspiring as you've convinced yourself that you are not.

TRY THIS: Have Playdates with Yourself

When you reconnect with your authentic self, you also rediscover who you were as a child. In other words, who you are at your core, before all that conditioning and growing up. What better way to strengthen that connection with your inner child than to let go of your adult worries and just have fun?

Every Labor Day weekend, my husband and I go to the Malibu Kiwanis Chili Cook-Off. And no, we don't go for the chili. We go for the Ferris wheel, the chocolate-dipped bananas, the carnival games, and the rides that make us dizzy. Why? Because it's important to have fun and enjoy life. We don't know how long we'll exist on this planet, so when we can indulge in life, we must treat each day as a gift.

So, at least once a month, do something fun for yourself! Try something that you've always wanted to do but just haven't found the day to do it. Go indoor skydiving, have a bowling night with friends, try that haunted house you've always wanted to go to, or spend an entire afternoon playing in that park by your home that you've only walked by and never enjoyed. Whatever you decide, just make sure it's something that is fun for *you.*

TRY THIS: Explore Some Personality Tests

For those of us who really love logic and science, research-based personality tests are a great way to boost your self-awareness. The following tests have varying degrees of depth, but they comprise some of my favorite of all time. I encourage you to explore the tests below and dive into learning more about what makes you *you*:

- **The Myers-Briggs Type Indicator (MBTI):** One of the most popular personality tests ever designed, the MBTI is based on a theory proposed by Carl Jung that there are four principal psychological functions through which we experience life. Within these four functions, you fall into one of two categories—Introverted or Extroverted, Intuitive or Sensing, Thinking or Feeling, and Perceiving or Judging—for a total of 16 different personality combinations. This is truly a fascinating test to take; many different companies and schools have even used it in recruitment. (Visit www.myersbriggs.org and www.MBTIonline.com for details.)

- **The Enneagram:** The Enneagram system consists of nine different personality types: the reformer, the helper, the achiever, the individualist, the investigator, the loyalist, the enthusiast, the challenger, and the peacemaker. Each type has a different pattern of thinking, feeling, and acting. (Visit enneagraminstitute.com for details.) Knowing your Enneagram personality type will help you identify unconscious patterns that trigger your reactions and influence your life. It can also help you discover untapped talents and abilities that may lead to your own self-actualization.

- **The Big Five:** The "Big Five" is also referred to as the International Personality Item Pool (IPIP) Big Five Factor Markers. This test measures what many psychologists consider to be the five major dimensions of personality: Openness, Conscientiousness, Agreeableness, Extraversion, and Neuroticism. (You can find a free version at Truity.com.)

Accept Your Flaws

"Remember, you have been criticizing yourself for years and it hasn't worked. Try approving of yourself and see what happens."

—Louise Hay

Now, before we go any further, there is something important we need to talk about. Remember how I mentioned that part of the choice to be imperfectly you involves learning to accept the aspects of yourself and your past that you aren't the biggest fan of? Let's face it. We're all human. We all have perceived flaws, we all make mistakes, and we all have past experiences we'd rather not talk about. But it's important to stop being so damn hard on ourselves and love our flaws.

Before you dive into loving your flaws, I thought I'd tell you one of mine.

The first 26 years of my life I was embarrassed of my heritage and ethnicity. My grandmother, who was my primary caregiver as I was growing up, always told me not to tell too many people I was Colombian. She told me to embrace the English language and immerse myself in American culture, and so I did as my grandmother said. Anyway, I didn't like being different, and almost all of the Latin kids I went to school with changed their names to sound more English than Spanish. (Think Roberto to Robert.) With a name like George, it was easy to downplay my Hispanic heritage and assert that I was "half German." (I wasn't lying either; my dad is actually German.)

On the other hand, my mother, Gloria Cansino, was damn proud of her heritage. She was a famous actress and professional dancer in Mexico until she met my father. She was always wearing Latin-inspired outfits and over-the-top Aztec costumes that would've rivaled Cher's outfits! Because my mother was raised in the entertainment industry, she missed out on normal childhood experiences. As an adult, she wasn't the type to cook and clean all day; she was a performer, after all! So my grandmother Maria fulfilled more of the traditional caregiver role, while my mother gave me love.

I was 26 years old when my mother passed away, and it triggered the realization that I had spent much of my past pretending to be someone I wasn't. Suddenly, all that she'd taught me about my heritage and her love for Latin culture resonated with me in a new, deeper way. Her death made me realize that I should be proud of my identity, and I suddenly felt a need to finally accept the parts of myself that I had denied, like my heritage. As I mentioned earlier, that's when I decided to change my name to Jorge to honor my mother and our Latin roots. I finally realized that there is nothing embarrassing about who I am, and I am extremely proud of my background and what it represents.

So, when it comes to you and your flaws, don't be afraid to embrace those imperfections that you've been hiding for your entire life. Those flaws aren't going away. They are a part of you. Ultimately, in order to love yourself, you must love your flaws.

The New Golden Rule

I know this may seem hard, but it's important to stop being so damn hard on ourselves. Do you remember the golden rule we were taught as kids? *Treat others how you want to be treated.* Well, I've found that we tend to treat others better than we treat ourselves. So my "golden" rule for you is this: *Treat yourself how you would treat others.* Think of someone whom you care about deeply. You don't see only their flaws, right? So stop judging yourself solely by your imperfections. Give yourself the love and respect you give everyone else.

I resisted the idea of embracing my imperfections for quite some time. As a total self-improvement junkie, I was convinced "fixing myself" was the way to freedom and happiness. After all, if you readily embrace your flaws, where's the motivation to change them? Isn't that a lazy way out? I've since discovered it's actually the very opposite. As Carl Jung said, "What you resist not only persists, but will grow in size." Accepting your imperfections brings about healing, which leads to the transformation you want.

Now, I'm not making a case against self-improvement. You can embrace your imperfections and still take the steps to improve. The key questions to ask yourself are:

- Can I do something about this?
- Do I want to?

If your flaw is something you *can* and *want to* do something about, go for it! Just remember to keep embracing and accepting along the way. If you can't and/or don't want to do something about it, the only answer is to embrace it.

If your perceived flaws are causing you harm, causing others harm, or interfering in your daily life, I encourage you to seek the added support of a therapist. You can still benefit greatly from this book by using the three choices in conjunction with your participation in one-on-one therapy or a support group. To find a therapist in your area, visit the American Psychological Association at locator.apa.org.

Embrace Your Imperfections

Think about one of your perceived imperfections for a second. For example, maybe you think you're too disorganized or scatterbrained. Maybe your nail-biting habit disgusts you, you consider your cellulite evil, or you think you're too moody. Anything goes!

Pretend I'm sitting next to you and tell me what's wrong with this flaw. Let it rip! Tell me how much you hate it. You might say something like this: "Jorge, I have the worst flaw. I'm so disorganized. I can't get anything done. Last night, I forgot to finish the laundry. My house is a total disaster, and I can't find anything. I just hate myself for being this way."

How did that make you feel? Notice how, in our example, being "too disorganized" snowballed into a massive problem? The more you resisted and rejected that part of you, the bigger of an issue it became. And the more it grew, the less empowered you felt. In fact, I'd be willing to bet you started to feel pretty powerless to change it.

Now let's take the same perceived imperfection and just embrace it. Seriously! I'm still sitting next to you, so go ahead and tell me how you've accepted this. For example: "Jorge, I'm disorganized, and that's okay. I'm human. I'm doing the best I can."

Notice how that took so much pressure off? How suddenly being "too" disorganized is no big deal at all? How much better and empowered you feel about yourself and how taking steps to improve actually feel a little possible?

Which approach will bring you closer to what you really want: a life that brings you those positive emotions you want to feel? Which approach is more likely to make you feel capable of real change and inspire you to take the steps to create that change?

Bingo! Embracing your imperfections!

TRY THIS: Pair Affirmations with Your Breath

Make a list of what you've always thought of as imperfections or negative qualities. For example:

- I'm disorganized.

- I'm unworthy.

- I'm too short.

- I'm too sensitive.

- I'm not good at socializing with large groups of people.

Now, next to each of your negative judgments, rewrite it as a positive quality. You can be as serious or as silly as you want. For example:

- I'm disorganized = I'm a free spirit, or I love my free-spirited, go-with-the-flow nature.

- I'm unworthy = I'm worthy, amazing, and loved!

- I'm too short = I'm petite and totally adorable, or I love that I never have to worry about towering over a date!

- I'm too sensitive = I love my sensitive, caring nature.

- I'm not good socializing in groups = I have an amazing ability to connect intimately and give my attention to one person.

Connecting the Dots

To this day, I have moments where I need to pause and remember that I'm not the weak person that my very domineering grandmother insisted I was. She shaped my early sense of self so that I was dependent and lacking in any real confidence. In addition to her constantly reminding me I wasn't a "*maricón*," she bathed me until I was 12 and didn't let me play with other kids. As a result, I was a very shy child who was not able to understand that this reality wasn't reflective of the world around me. It wasn't until I went to college that I was able to begin to break free from some of this influence, but it still shadowed me for many more years. It wasn't until I was 39 that I started to own my true identity as a gay man.

But, if given the option, would I go back and choose a different upbringing?

Nope.

My past has played a role in who I am. I'm grateful for it. Although my grandmother was hard on me, I know that she wanted the best for me, even though she sometimes chose a misguided way to demonstrate her love. All that I went through made me who I am today, which eventually even allowed me to find my soul mate and husband, Sam. *Everything happens for a reason.* Instead of trying to rewrite history, we must learn from it and create a better future.

Now, I didn't always feel this way. I spent many years working through all that early programming and reestablishing my sense of self, sometimes with the help of professional therapists. There was one major lesson that transformed everything, though.

One night, I had just finished an intense workout at the gym and was feeling motivated to make peace with past. So I did what most of us probably do when faced with a problem: I Googled some possible solutions. Now, when I search for inspiration, I often look to public speeches, and that night I found a 2005 Stanford University commencement speech from Steve Jobs. This speech finally made everything click for me. You might say that it turned my past from lemons to lemonade.

Steve's first story in the speech was about connecting the dots of your life. He explained: "[You] can't connect the dots looking forward; you can only connect them looking backward. So you have to trust that the dots will somehow connect in your future. You have to trust in something—your gut, destiny, life, karma, whatever. This approach has never let me down, and it has made all the difference in my life." This really resonated with me and allowed me to look at all the obstacles of my life as a map to my future. Those hurdles that I had hated jumping over were the same hurdles that got me to where I am today, and I wouldn't change a thing.

While we can't go back and magically redo the past, we can go back and change the *meaning* we give our past experiences, whether it's childhood pain, our own guilt, or regrets we have. We change the story we tell ourselves.

TRY THIS: Changing History

This exercise will help you gain perspective on your own story and help you connect the dots within your own life, so that you can see every moment has its own purpose. Read the following exercise description below, and then write in your story in a journal, tablet, or computer.

Pretend that you're 100 years old. Energetic as ever in mind, body, and spirit, you've created exactly the life you want. You've been invited to give the commencement speech at a well-known university, and the topic will be: "How my past allowed me to learn and grow."

Think of something in your past that caused you pain: a childhood difficulty, regret, mistake, betrayal, difficult person, etc. Now, you're going to use that experience to tell a new story, one that inspires these young people who are about to go into the world. (The key word is *inspire!* Remember, these college kids are filled with trepidation and uncertainty. Plus, many are now carrying tons of debt. They need a pick-me-up!)

Write your commencement speech. Tell them how this experience helped you grow and develop strength you didn't know you had. Explain how it made you into who you are, and how, as horrible as it was, something good came out of it.

Reveal and Live
the Best You

"Where there is no struggle, there is no strength."

— Oprah Winfrey

Now that you've learned how to embody the real you and embrace the imperfect you, here is where we focus on revealing the *best* version of you. There are two keys to this. The first is to master the stories you tell yourself, and the second is to affirm your best you.

Your Thinking Literally Changes Your Brain

Scientists are now certain that our brains are ever-changing, and, thanks to brain scan studies, we can see how the brain's neural pathways are continuously shifting and reorganizing. The brain's neural pathways are what connect the different areas of the brain and transmit messages. Different neural pathways are responsible for different behaviors and emotions. Through a process known as neuroplasticity, your brain is actually capable of forming brand-new neural pathways, and the best part is you can direct some of this change through your consciousness!

In one fascinating study published in the *Journal of Neurophysiology*, participants were asked to play a basic series of piano notes every day for five days. Another group of participants were asked to *imagine* playing the same notes every day for five days. Both groups had their brains scanned every day, which revealed that the changes in the brains of those who imagined playing the piano were the same as those who actually played the piano. This study shows not only that the way you think has the power to change your brain— talk about power—but also that your brain can't tell the difference between what is real and what you are just imagining!

As brain researcher Joe Dispenza says in his fascinating book *Evolve Your Brain*: "What is so amazing about our brain and the frontal lobe is that we have the ability to make a thought become the only thing that is real to us . . . When we make our thoughts all that is real and pay attention to them as if they were, we unite the frontal lobe's primary functions into a force as powerful as anything in the universe."

In essence, you have enormous power at your fingertips. Don't doubt the power that's within. You can actually think your way to your best, most authentic, most extraordinary you . . . and create what you want in your life.

You Can Choose Your Thoughts

When you think about it, most of us go through our day on autopilot, doing what needs to get done, totally unaware of our thinking. Yet our minds are buzzing around in the background, going from thought to thought, all of which are reminding us what we have to do, telling us who we are, recalling experiences from the past, and so on. In fact, it's been estimated that some 60,000 thoughts enter our mind each day. And, according to the Cleveland Clinic, some 95 percent of those thoughts are the same ones repeated every day—and 80 percent of those are negative. Yikes!

Those thoughts are also triggering all sorts of corresponding emotions. But by consciously choosing certain thoughts, you can actually change your emotions. As Joe Dispenza describes in *Evolve Your Brain*: "Your every thought produces a biochemical reaction in the brain. The brain then releases chemical signals that are transmitted to the body, where they act as messengers of the thought. The thoughts that produce the chemicals in the brain allow your body to *feel* exactly the way you are *thinking*. So every thought produces a chemical that is matched by a feeling in your body. Essentially, when you think happy, inspiring, or positive thoughts, your brain manufactures chemicals that make you feel joyful, inspired, or uplifted."

I know, the idea of changing your thoughts sounds hokey and difficult. You might be thinking, *This is all fascinating, Jorge. I get it. I'd love to do this. But I don't have the time or energy to take control of 60,000 thoughts.*

Guess what? This isn't about taking control of every single thought. You're human—remember?—and it's okay to be imperfect. Thoughts will come and go. There will be negative ones, and that's okay.

The key to a happy life is to question the thoughts that aren't working for you, thereby reducing their power, and introduce new, more positive ones. Remember every single thought triggers an emotion as well as a domino reaction of corresponding emotions. So every time you take one little step toward a negative thought, no matter how small, you're going to get a result of corresponding negative thoughts and emotions. On the other hand, every time you take a step toward a positive thought, you'll get corresponding positive thoughts and emotions!

So in the following sections, you'll learn simple yet incredibly effective techniques for taking the reins on your thinking and affirming the best you.

TRY THIS: Don't Believe Everything You Think

Bring to mind some of the negative beliefs you have about yourself. As much as you might be convinced nobody likes you, as much as you tell yourself you're not capable, and as much as you know there's something wrong with you . . . all those thoughts are just in your mind. As we discussed, however, the problem is that your mind can't tell the difference between outer reality and a thought you have about it. Every time you have a negative thought, you are building that neural pathway and reinforcing that belief.

For example, I used to constantly tell myself that I was weak and not capable. I also grew up repeating that mantra, "Tu no eres maricón." The more I had these thoughts, the more I believed them, the more I built up those neural pathways, and the more I embodied them as who I was.

I've since learned that the key to letting go of a thought is to create space between you and the thought. It's kind of like putting a wall up between yourself and those thoughts. The best way I've found to do so is to question it through a revolutionary technique called The Work, developed by spiritual pioneer Byron Katie.

As part of doing The Work, Katie suggests you ask four specific questions about the thought that is causing you suffering. They are:

1. Is this true? (Yes or no. If no, move to 3.)

2. Can you absolutely know that it's true? (Yes or no.)

3. How do you react, what happens, when you believe that thought?

4. Who would you be without the thought?

Now ask yourself these questions with a negative belief that you hold about yourself. I highly recommend doing The Work any time you have a negative thought.

Choose Positive Self-Affirmations to Reprogram Your Brain

An affirmation is a statement about yourself or your experience, phrased in the present tense as if it were true. Positive affirmations are truly the most powerful tool for connecting with and embodying your best self. As Louise Hay, one of the pioneers of positive thinking and the use of affirmations, says, "The thoughts we choose to think are the tools we use to paint the canvas of our lives."

Through the use of this form of positive self-talk, you're able to take some control of your consciousness and introduce new thoughts, which will help shape your brain and trigger corresponding emotions. Remember, the brain doesn't know what's real or not. In the same way that you can reinforce negative thoughts about yourself, you can use positive affirmations to create new neural pathways and reprogram your brain.

The idea of affirmations may be completely new to you, or you may be well versed in their use. Whether or not you need convincing on the efficacy of this method, the latest studies on their effectiveness across all areas of our lives are remarkable. For example, positive self-affirmation has been shown to:

- *Improve self-confidence and social confidence.* In a study published in *Psychological Science*, researchers found that the use of self-affirmation improved confidence and made individuals more comfortable in social interactions. They also found by practicing affirmations for just 15 minutes a week, the effects of that initial 15 minutes of self-affirmation last up to two months.

- *Boost performance.* In a recent study published by the *Journal of Personality and Social Psychology*, researchers found that people who feel inadequate can boost their performance and power through self-affirmations. Participants who affirmed their greatest job strengths and traits operated with more confidence when in high-pressure situations.

- *Improve problem solving under stress.* In another study, published in *PLOS ONE*, researchers found that self-affirmation can improve problem solving and creativity during times of stress. Acute and chronic stress has been shown to impair performance and decrease academic achievement. Researchers chose participants with perceived chronic stress and randomly assigned half of them to practice a self-affirmation. They were then tested on 30 different problem-solving items under time constraints. The results showed that self-affirmation improved problem-solving performance under stress.

- *Improve willpower.* In one study published in the *Journal of Personality and Social Psychology*, researchers found that self-affirmations can improve willpower and self-control. Participants who affirmed their core values operated with more determination and self-control than those participants who did not use self-affirmation exercises.

When you choose positive affirmations to reprogram your brain, it's important to make sure that they're aligned with your authentic self. That is why I'm excited to share with you an all-new technique for creating a series of very powerful custom affirmations that will help you quickly embody your best you. I call this your Happy Code.

Your Happy Code

Years ago, I believed that anyone could be and do absolutely anything they wanted. I still believe that—within reason. But, let's face it, there are some things that just aren't "you." Throughout my years working in the transformation industry, I've found that again and again we're affirming who we feel we *should* be, instead of who we *are*. The more we affirm those shoulds, the more disconnected we feel and the more we reject our true selves. As a result, we lose our personal power.

I spent the first 39 years of my life affirming I wasn't gay, but I was gay. Yes, that is a more extreme situation, but this use of affirming the shoulds extends to all areas. My client Cindy, for example, desperately wants to be a size zero. Even after losing tons of weight and looking amazing as a size four, she's fixated on being a certain size. Yet the more she affirms that she wants to be a size zero, the worse she feels—and the more she wants to eat as a coping mechanism.

Another client, Adam, thinks he should be a manager at his company. After all, it sounds so much better than "associate." Yet he's a highly creative, introverted man who loves to buckle down behind a closed office door. Although he can continue to affirm that he is a manager and strive for that in his life, chances are that he'd be much happier working on his own rather than leading a team.

How do we break this pattern of affirming our shoulds? The key is to use affirmations that are in line with your most powerful authentic self, the imperfect you. With the following quiz, you will be able to assess your authentic tendencies. Once you understand what resonates with your true self, you will be able to choose positive affirmations that reinforce your best you—not just positive affirmations that reinforce who you think you *should* be. These are the affirmations that make up your "Happy Code": your unique blueprint for affirming what makes up your authentic self.

TRY THIS: Identify Your Happy Code

Read the statements in each column and choose the ones that you connect with immediately. Your answer should feel most you—the choice that feels like freedom.

For each aspect of the Happy Code, I've included affirmations to help reinforce your authentic tendencies. Choose the affirmations that resonate with you.

YOUR ENERGY CODE: CALM *OR* FIRE

I can easily sit and work for hours.	I fidget and find it hard to sit still during the day.
I prefer to play a supporting, rather than "starring," role.	I often find myself at events in which I am the center of attention.
I take each task as it comes. I plan my schedules with plenty of space.	I thrive when I have a lot of things on my to-do list.
I've been described as having an "old soul," deep thoughts, or a creative mind.	I've been described as passionate, fiery, and emotional.
I believe that things tend to work themselves out.	I operate at a quick tempo and can become impatient if I am slowed down.

If you resonate with more statements in column A, you have calm energy.

- *I am an island of calm energy. Others appreciate my soothing presence.*

- *During times of chaos, I breathe deeply and remember that all is well.*

- *My creativity and insight are welcome additions to any situation.*

If you resonate with more statements in column B, you have fire energy.

- *I always have enough energy for any task that I wish to undertake.*

- *My joyful presence enlivens every situation. It is fun to be me!*

- *I serve the world by bringing passion to everything I do.*

YOUR CONTROL CODE: PASSIVE *OR* ACTIVE

It's more fun to be a passenger in a car than the driver.	I prefer to be the driver in a car rather than the passenger.
In the workplace, I enjoy executing tasks that I am given.	I enjoy being a leader and teaching others new skills.
I believe in destiny; I trust in the path that is meant for me.	I believe that I am in charge of my own fate.
I am drawn to leaders and decisive people who know what they want.	I am drawn to people who can take direction and execute my vision.
If any obstacle appears, I patiently wait for it to work itself out.	I prefer to be the person who makes final decisions.

If you resonate with more statements in column A, you prefer passive control.

- *I go with the flow, set my worries aside, and let life unfold as it will.*

- *The energy of the universe works through me.*

- *My patience and understanding are wonderful assets in every situation.*

If you resonate with more statements in column B, you prefer active control.

- *I am in control of my own life. I make smart, calculated plans for my future.*

- *When I take charge, things run smoothly. Leading others is a responsibility and a delight.*

- *My clear vision of the future helps others find their own direction.*

YOUR ATTACHMENT CODE:
COOPERATIVE *OR* INDEPENDENT

It's more fun to eat with others, whether it's at a dinner party or a restaurant.	I prefer to eat what I want, when I want, rather than making plans with others.
I sometimes use shopping as an excuse for spending time with friends.	I like to shop alone and efficiently. When shopping with a group, we often split up.
The idea of traveling alone sounds dull, frightening, or uninteresting to me.	The idea of traveling alone sounds like an exciting adventure.
When I feel run-down, I seek out the company of family or friends.	When I need to recharge, I find a place where I can be alone.
I prefer being a part of a team and collaborating with others.	I enjoy working independently and without the help of others.

If you resonate with more statements in column A, you have cooperative attachment.

- *I am energized by the company of my family and friends, and they enjoy my presence as well.*

- *I appreciate different viewpoints, knowing that multiple options are equally wonderful. Cooperating with others is a joy.*

- *Being in a crowd is fun for me. Every stranger is an opportunity to make a new, incredible friend.*

If you resonate with more statements in column B, you have independent attachment.

- *I am important. I allow myself to prioritize my own needs and desires.*

- *When I take time to care for myself, my example inspires others to do the same.*

- *I deeply love and accept myself.*

YOUR INTIMACY CODE:
OPEN *OR* RESERVED

I enjoy discussing my life and feelings with new acquaintances.	I prefer to get to know someone before sharing my emotions.
I don't really have a "poker face." You can usually read my thoughts on my face.	I always appear calm and collected when in public.
I sometimes say the first thing that comes to my mind.	I think carefully about the words I choose before speaking with others.
I am proud of my life and never want to hide it.	I get embarrassed easily. It's better not to speak than to share too much information.
I believe honesty is always the best policy for communication.	I believe that sometimes it's best not to reveal everything to to everyone.

If you resonate with more statements in column A, you have open energy.

- *My open, honest energy is a wonderful asset in all situations.*

- *When I offer trust, others love and accept me for who I am.*

- *I live my truth. I am free to be me!*

If you resonate with more statements in column B, you have reserved energy.

- *Every situation benefits from my thoughtfulness and careful actions.*

- *I set strong boundaries as a way of showing respect to others as well as myself.*

- *My energy is a valuable resource that I gladly spend when it feels right to do so.*

YOUR SPIRITUAL CODE:
TRUSTING *OR* SKEPTICAL

I believe in a higher power and trust that there is a path that was paved for me.	I believe that most things can be understood through logic and reason.
Having a spiritual path is important to me.	Honesty and truth are important to me.
There is much wisdom to be gained from religious texts and leaders.	There are multiple paths to explore. No one person or faith has all the answers.
I sometimes make decisions based on signs from above and my own gut feelings.	I wait until I have all the evidence before deciding to commit to something.
I trust people to be honest and easily put my faith in others.	I value my trust and see it as something that needs to be earned.

If you resonate with more statements in column A, you are trusting on your spiritual path.

- *I look within and above for answers.*

- *I trust in the universe and know that all is well.*

- *My spiritual path is rewarding. My faith brings me peace.*

If you resonate with more statements in column B, you are skeptical on your spiritual path.

- *My inquisitive mind takes me on wonderful journeys. I love to learn!*

- *I am competent and self-reliant. I trust myself to research the answer to any questions that I have.*

- *My mind is open to many ideas. As I explore different paths, I remain cautious and skeptical in my quest for the truth.*

Your Rx:
Everyday Being

"Here is the crux of the matter, the distilled essence, the only thing you need to remember: When considering whether to say yes or no, you must choose the response that feels like freedom. Period."

— Martha Beck

Should I get out of bed yet? Should I have oatmeal or Cheerios for breakfast? Should I wear my new jeans or work khakis today? Should I make lunch for my sons or have them make it themselves? Should I go to that business meeting in New York next week even though I am extremely jet-lagged? What work project should I prioritize today? Should I meet up with that friend who always seems to bring me down? Do I want to stay in with my husband tonight or go out with our friends we haven't seen in a while?

So many choices, so little time! So how do you know when you're making a decision that's in line with your imperfect, authentic self—your best you?

Any time you're unsure what to do, take a deep breath and go with what makes you feel free. Whether you're deciding what to have for dinner or what job to take, the "right" choice (the one that's aligned with your imperfect you) will feel like freedom. I can think of no story that better illustrates this point than Martha Beck's.

Choosing Freedom

I met Martha in 2002, when I had been invited by Liz Brody, an editor for *O, The Oprah Magazine*, to do a photo shoot in New York City to promote my book *8 Minutes in the Morning*. When I arrived at the shoot, Martha was already there, taking some new head shots. I love to hear people's stories, so I asked Martha hers. Little did I know that Martha had gone on her own quest to find an authentic life.

Martha's journey included an abusive upbringing, being raised Mormon, having a child with Down syndrome, and marrying a man who later realized he was gay—only to realize subsequently that she too was gay. These revelations caused her to be rejected by her religion. After Martha found the courage overcome her limiting beliefs about what creates happiness, she was then able to leave the Mormon church, divorce her husband, face the abuse she'd suffered as a child, and accept her truth of being gay. And then? Then she became an even better version of herself than she'd ever dreamed of.

At the time, I wasn't out, nor was I questioning my sexuality; my marriage was strong and my career was fruitful. But Martha's story really resonated with me. It planted a seed inside me that, although neglected for seven years, would one day grow to fruition. In fact, on the day my employee asked me when I was coming out, I thought about how Martha's life seemed so similar to my own. I did a quick Google search to see what Martha was up to and found an interview with her in the *Guardian*. It reminded me that we make the choice to live the life we want.

In her interview, Martha said: "Most of the time we're off-centre, and we don't feel quite right, so we're always seeking something. We think certain things will give it to us, most of them culturally defined—a lot of money, a bigger house, whatever. Those usually don't fulfill the need, so we keep looking. You play your life like a game of 'getting warmer, getting colder,' consistently making choices that make you happier in a deep way." This was exactly how *I* was feeling on the inside. The difference is that Martha kept looking until she found a life that was *right for her.*

Today, Martha is a best-selling author of several books as well as a columnist for *O, The Oprah Magazine* (and has been since its inception in 2001). She recently appeared at The Chopra Center and gives lectures all around the globe that help millions of people create what she refers to as "their right life." Martha untangled what seemed to be an extremely complicated life situation—talk about finding simplicity and freedom, not to mention honoring the small voice that speaks to your deep inner soul.

Whenever you feel like your day isn't going quite the way you want, come back to this story and remember that *you* are in control of your life.

Affirmations: The Key to Unlocking Your Inner Self

Affirmations are key to truly embodying your authentic self and living your best you. Use the ones from your Happy Code as inspiration to create your own. Also, look back at the emotion wheel in the beginning of this book and try to come up with affirmations that reflect what you really want to feel.

Add affirmations into your daily routine and surround yourself with these thoughts. The more you surround yourself with positive, loving thoughts that affirm the best version of your authentic self, the more you evolve. I tell myself my affirmations every day, and they help me remind myself how much I love me!

The following tips will help you incorporate affirmations into your daily life to help you reconnect with your authentic self, accept your flaws, and live as your best you:

- Choose your favorite affirmations and repeat them out loud for five minutes, three times a day. (Ideally, morning, lunch, and before bed.)

- Write your favorite affirmations in a journal three times a day.

- Make a recording of yourself reading your favorite affirmations and listen to it while driving. For the recording, I recommend saying each affirmation at least two times in a row, so that you can first listen, and then repeat the affirmation with yourself.

- Make cards with your favorite affirmations on them. Put them in areas where you'll frequently see them, such as on your computer, on the fridge, in your closet, or next to the light switch.

- Every day, choose one affirmation to focus on. Repeat it every time you open a door or look in the mirror.

How to Start: Your 4-Week Practice

Don't know where to begin with being imperfectly you? Consider doing the following for the next four weeks.

Week 1: Start a journal and write in it every day for a week. You can write about how your day went, what you hope to accomplish from reading this book or anything you want—all you have to do is write it down.

Week 2: Make a list of your imperfections and write them down in your journal. For the next week, I want you to designate five minutes each day to accepting these imperfections out loud. For example, if one of your imperfections is that you are overweight, you will say, "For these five minutes, it's all right to be exactly as I am. I love my body." Think of this as a five-minute vacation to release your anxiety and nonacceptance.

Week 3: Say affirmations for ten minutes each day. Pick the affirmations that you most identify with in your Happy Code and say them to yourself for ten minutes each day this week. Don't be afraid to repeat the affirmations again and again; repetition is key to affirmations.

Week 4: Face your affirmations! Say them in front of a mirror for 10 minutes each day this week. Repeat the affirmations you used from Week 3, but also come up with five new affirmations you would like to say to yourself and include those in your daily practice. Think of other ways to incorporate your favorite affirmations into your daily life this week: write in your journal; record your favorites; make cards to put on your mirror, in your car, or on your desk at work.

Congratulations! You now have the power to embody your imperfect you anytime, anywhere, thanks to the simple tools laid out in this chapter. With your growing self-awareness and self-acceptance, you're bound to feel more comfortable in your own skin. You are now also armed with one of the simplest, most power-ful tools to instantly change your mood, change your biochemistry, and become your best you: your custom Happy Code.

Now it's time to slow down a bit and take a breather with the next simple choice. . .

CHOICE 2
Don't Hold Your Breath

"If you want to conquer the anxiety of life, live in the moment, live in the breath."

— Amit Ray

Don't hold your breath. My youngest son was the most recent person to tell me this. We had just sat down to a delicious dinner cooked by my husband, Sam. Parker, my oldest son, was chatting away about surf camp and the latest happenings in seventh grade. I glanced over and caught Owen, my youngest child, gingerly eating around his broccoli (as usual—just like any other nine-year-old would).

Being the health-conscious dad that I am, I suggested to Owen (as usual) that he try it. "Dad, don't hold your breath," he replied. Owen cracks me up so much—little did he know that his funny catchphrase carries profound wisdom.

Your breath *is* life. Every breath you take gives you a new lease on life; your life is happening in this very moment thanks to the inhale you just took. It's not happening yesterday, it's not happening tomorrow or a year from now. It's happening *now.* Yet so many of us aren't giving ourselves that full power of breath—instead, we're holding our breath, putting our lives on pause, living in the past, or waiting for something to happen—whether it's my son eating broccoli or you finally meeting the One. (I'm still not giving up on him trying broccoli, though!)

Although breathing is an automatic body function that is subconsciously controlled by the brain stem, you can also take some conscious control of it. In other words, you can choose *how* you breathe or you can choose to let your breath run on autopilot 100 percent of the time. The unconscious choice usually involves poor and shallow breathing. Breathing better and more mindfully can lead to an array of health benefits, such as higher energy, less stress, more open emotions, improved blood pressure, and better sleep. This one simple yet unbelievably powerful choice energizes, calms, and balances you mentally, physically, and spiritually. It also enables you to access the only thing that exists right now— this present moment—which is your special sweet spot for all life transformation.

These are all the reasons the second choice to free yourself from whatever is holding you back is . . . don't hold your breath.

First, let me tell you a story of mine that demonstrates the limitless potential of breath.

Panic to Power

I'd been sitting on my cold, checkered bathroom floor for what seemed like an eternity . . . At least, it was an eternity for someone who is usually upbeat and always on the go. I had recently separated from my wife and come out to her about being attracted to men. (Even after the separation, it took me months to actually be able to say the words "I'm gay" without feeling sick to my stomach.) I had moved down the street to a quiet and quaint beach house, where everything felt so foreign to me. I'd thought this move would give me some space so I could find clarity on who I was and what I wanted, but instead, all I felt was sheer panic. My chest felt tight, as if it were carrying the weight of the world, and I could barely breathe.

I'd spent the better part of the week feeling like this, roaming around the all-too-quiet house, my heartbeat almost audible. *Aren't breakups supposed to lead to a personal self-discovery quest, à la* Eat, Pray, Love? I thought, half-jokingly. *Maybe I should have followed Elizabeth Gilbert's lead and gone to Italy, India, and Bali instead.*

I thought to myself, *How could I be gay? What is wrong with me?* I felt as if I had just been told I had cancer, one that would disable me for the rest of my life. Furthermore, the career I had worked so hard for was in serious jeopardy; at this point in time, the world wasn't as accepting to homosexuality as it is today. I believed that if I came out, all my clients, fans, and business connections would disown me like a leper. I didn't even *want* to have a career anymore. I didn't want to see my friends. In fact, I didn't want to do anything—I didn't want to live my life anymore.

2:38 A.M. . . . That's what the clock said. It was late, but I needed to talk to someone. I had been crying on the bathroom floor for hours. So I called my best friend, my wife. I told her that I had hit what I thought was rock bottom, depressed and all alone. She reassured me that we were always going to be close, that I was going to be okay. For a few seconds I believed her, but I couldn't stop feeling like a corpse on the inside. Every day, I would wake up and not want to open my eyes or even think about moving out of bed. For those of you who know me or have seen me on television before, you know that I am not a weak, sad, low-energy person. I'm a Latin celebrity trainer who's loud, motivated, and always positive. But during this time, I felt so broken, so unclear on what my life would become.

I was incredibly scared for my own life, so I called my person, my rock, my sister Marta. She told me to repeat three words to her: "All is well." I repeated those words with tears in my eyes and my breath clenched. I didn't believe what I saying, nor did I think it would help. After an hour of my crying on the phone to her, she declared that she was moving in with me for a few weeks, just so I had someone for support.

Over the next two weeks, Marta took care of me. She took all the photos off the walls and put Post-its everywhere so that my home was fully redecorated with positive affirmations and quotes. (Full disclosure: my house looked like I was a conspiracy theorist on the brink of a breakthrough.) But the most important thing she did was teach me how to breathe for what seemed like the first time in my life.

Over the next couple weeks, Marta and I did nothing but breathe and affirm the positive words that surrounded us on every corner of my house. You'll find some of the exercises we did in this chapter, including belly breathing, boost breathing, and slow diaphragmatic breathing. These techniques really helped me overcome one of the hardest times in my life; I finally felt like I could feel my lungs again. Suddenly, all the panic and fear that had been disabling me didn't seem so astronomical anymore. I accepted that my sexuality was not a disease; instead, it was a part of me. It was a part of what made up Jorge Cruise.

This was the turning point for me. It may sound so simple—but remember that I said the choices were simple! With each breath, I felt more powerful, more calm, more myself, and more capable of rising above challenges that lay in front of me. I felt more of what I *really* wanted—all those positive feelings I ultimately wanted to feel. Just a few months later, I found the courage to embrace all of who I was at my deepest core and tell the world I was gay.

That is the quiet power of breath, affirmations, and embracing your authentic self. (See how well Choices 1 and 2 work together?) No matter what is happening, you can use your breath to change your conscious state in an instant and give you the strength to remember who you are and turn things around.

•••

So are you ready to breathe your way to a better life? By the end of this chapter, you'll know exactly how to tap into the transformational power of your breath. You'll learn how to use your breath to practice mindfulness and connect with the present moment. I'll also teach you several innovative breathing techniques that you can effortlessly incorporate into your life right now, all of which bring about instant results. Here's our road map for the coming pages:

- *Become mindful of your breath.* Here I'll teach you how to use your breath to release obsessive thoughts and stress and connect with the present moment, which is your sweet spot for creating what you really want in your life.

- *The benefits of better breathing.* In this section, I'll give you a comprehensive overview of all the ways breathing better affects your brain and body and improves your health and well-being.

- *Better breathing techniques.* Here I share the breathing exercises I personally use. These are fun, easy, and instantly make you feel more balanced, energized, and strong.

- *Your Rx: Everyday breathing.* In this section, we'll talk about how you can easily and effortlessly incorporate better breathing into your everyday life.

The first step to take to unleash the power of your breath is to simply become *aware* of it.

Become Mindful of Your Breath

"Give yourself permission to allow this moment to be exactly as it is, and allow yourself to be exactly as you are."

— Dr. Jon Kabat-Zinn

Think about how your mind typically works throughout the day. Upon waking, if you're lucky you have a few moments where you get to savor your comfy bed. That's you putting your awareness on the present. Then you notice the time and think about how you have to get up, then comes a flood of stressful thoughts about all the things you have to do today. As you make breakfast, maybe you burn your toast, which leads to you feeling frustrated with yourself for not changing the toaster setting. Then as you head out the door, you're thinking about the presentation you have to give at work. Your phone rings—it's your mother, and the last conversation you had with her didn't go well. Next thing you know, you've veered off into running an imaginary angry dialogue with your mother, during which you tell her exactly what you think. This imaginary conversation fades in and out of your mind during the entire drive to work, save for the occasional thought about the presentation you're nervous about and those few moments at the stoplight when you admire the man in the car behind you through your rearview mirror. Then you get to work and on and on it goes. Thoughts come and go, back and forth, in and out, like the waves of an ocean. Before you know it, you're getting ready for bed and another day has come and gone.

It all sounds exhausting, right? That's where mindfulness comes in.

Mindfulness is the practice of bringing your complete attention to the present moment. When you're mindful, you are simply observing, without judgment, the ongoing stream of internal and external stimuli as they come and go. This may seem so basic, but it's actually a very powerful process.

The Benefits of Mindfulness

By nature, our minds tend to go into overdrive, deviating onto obsessive thoughts about the past or future, which then leads to stress and anxiety. It's like a bad habit; we don't mean to do it, we just do it because we're human. The practice of mindfulness allows you to detach from all those thoughts and just allow them to go in and out of your mind without your reacting to them.

When you're mindful, you connect with this very moment, which is your ultimate point of power for changing anything. The past is gone. The future is yet to be determined. Now is all you have, and it's only in this now that you have the power to create what you really want.

The principles of mindfulness (particularly in meditation) have been used by various cultures and religions for centuries, and modern psychologists have long used the practice of mindfulness as a way to help a variety of mental and physical conditions. In the '70s, Dr. Jon Kabat-Zinn, a researcher at the University of Massachusetts Medical School, brought the practice and its profound benefits into the mainstream.

Research studies have shown that people who practice mindfulness can experience a plethora of benefits, including:

- Reduced stress
- Improved memory

- Reduced depression

- Improved cognitive flexibility

- Reduced anxiety

- Increased relationship satisfaction

- Improved focus

- Decreased desire to binge eat

- Decreased use of substances such as alcohol, cigarettes, and drugs

- Reduction in tendency to ruminate

Having personally practiced mindfulness for years, I can attest to its benefits. As someone with a *very* busy mind, mindfulness has personally helped me detach from my stressful thoughts and find happiness in the moment.

Mindful Breathing

Now, what does all this have to do with breathing? Well, the simple act of focusing on your breath is one of the easiest ways to practice mindfulness. From the moment you're born to the moment you die, you breathe. It's always happening in the background, no matter what is happening in your life. So in many ways it's the most natural tool for mindfulness.

Many meditation techniques, including those based on the Zen Buddhist tradition, harness the power of breathing to help bring one's attention and focus to the present. Traditional mindfulness meditation is practiced by sitting cross-legged, with your back straight and eyes closed. Awareness is put on your breath as it goes in and out of the nostrils and lungs. If your awareness becomes distracted by outside influences, you must refocus on the movement of breath in and out of the body.

In his acclaimed book *Full Catastrophe Living*, mindfulness expert Dr. Jon Kabat-Zinn so beautifully describes the experience of mindful breathing:

> When we are mindful of our breathing, it helps us to calm the body and the mind. Then we are able to be aware of our thoughts and feelings with a greater degree of calmness and with a more discerning eye. We are able to see things more clearly and with a larger perspective, all because we are a little more awake, a little more aware. And with this awareness comes a feeling of having more room to move, of having more options, of being free to choose effective and appropriate responses in stressful situations rather than losing our equilibrium and sense of self as a result of feeling overwhelmed, thrown off balance by our own knee-jerk reactions.

Many of the benefits of breathing, which you will learn about in the next section, also coincide with the benefits of meditation and mindfulness. In fact, the specific breathing techniques that you will learn in this chapter draw from a long and rich tradition of meditative techniques. By bringing your focus to your breath, you are implementing the key components of meditation in a way that allows you to quickly feel the benefits from this type of mindfulness practice.

So if you want more calm, more freedom, and more balance, dive in and give it a shot! Here are all the details you need to breathe mindfully.

TRY THIS: Mindful Breathing Technique

Using your breath to practice mindfulness involves simply putting your focus on your breathing *just as it is*. Simply observe each inhale and exhale, without trying to change it. Let it come and go naturally. It's like riding a bike: don't think about it, just feel and be aware of your movement. When thoughts enter your mind (and they will), just let them come and go, as if each thought is a leaf swept up in the wind, just blowing past you.

Here's a step-by-step guide on how to do this:

- **Get into a comfortable position.** Sit in a chair or on the floor, in a comfortable place with little distraction. (Lying down is not ideal, as it's too tempting to fall asleep.)

- **Relax.** Take one deep breath to help relax your body, then just go back to breathing normally. You may also want to close your eyes. (I find this helps me focus, but it's not necessary.)

- **Tune in to your breath.** Feel each inhale and exhale, your chest and belly rising and falling. Remember, you don't need to think about breathing, just let the breaths come and go as they normally would.

- **Refocus.** When thoughts enter your mind, just let them go and refocus on the breath. You may on occasion get lost in a thought passing by. Don't beat yourself up. Just tune back in to the breath.

- **Continue.** Sit this way for five minutes, again just refocusing on the breath whenever you're distracted.

I recommend you do the preceding exercise once a day, if possible. You can also practice it anytime during your day. Whenever you're feeling stressed or down, just take a few minutes and focus on your breathing. Other times that make for easy reminders for you to practice your mindful breathing are a pause between tasks at work; becoming aware of your breath before you enter or leave a building; and counting out breaths before you reply to a verbal question, text, or e-mail. (Later in this chapter, I list my favorite apps that can help keep your breathing focused during the day.)

You'll be amazed at how effective this simple tool is, even if you do it for just a minute. It's like taking a free minivacation!

...

Now let's delve more into the act of breathing itself and cover some more ways you can tap into this underutilized transformational tool.

The Benefits of Better Breathing

*"Feelings come and go like clouds in a windy sky.
Conscious breathing is my anchor."*

— Thich Nhat Hanh

Obviously, you have to breathe to have any sort of life at all. It's the first thing you do when you come into this world, and it's the last thing you'll do before you leave it—but breathing is much more, or less, than that. It all depends on *how* you breathe.

I think of breathing as the perfect metaphor for life itself. Each inhale is a representation of fresh and new opportunities, a chance to be open-minded, willing, and connected to new experiences, while every exhale symbolizes the release of old and static ideas. Every cell in your body requires oxygen to function, and full breathing is how your body naturally detoxifies itself. Around 70 percent of the body's toxins are released when you exhale fully, *if* you inhale fully. If your life is shallow or superficial, then chances are, so is your breathing. The average human has a lung capacity of about six liters of air, but most of us don't use up that space.

Besides its ordinary and yet extremely important function of keeping you alive, breathing has several other functions for bettering your brain, your body, and your overall life, especially when you breathe better. I define *better breathing* as the act of inhaling fully and exhaling completely so that, with each inhale and exhale, your brain and body get the maximum effect and benefits from the air you breathe as well as the particular technique you're using. Better breathing is also knowing how you can use control to change your breath to address various situations and experiences that arise in your life.

Breathing and Your Brain

Practicing the breathing exercises in this chapter will improve your overall psychological profile: reducing stress, cooling down anger, and boosting happiness, as well as enhancing your ability to concentrate, focus, and remember. And did I mention that better breathing will make you better in the bedroom? Read on for details on all the brain benefits of breathing:

- **Feel happier and lower stress.** Breathing techniques can connect your body and mind by increasing the oxygen flow to your brain and stimulating a state of peace and calm. In addition, deep breathing can stop the release of cortisol, the stress hormone, which increases when we are anxious.

- **Feel blissed out.** Released from the pleasure centers of the brain, the neurotransmitter dopamine floods your brain when you practice deep breathing, resulting in an enhanced feeling of well-being and lower levels of depression.

- **Boost mood and lower stress.** Serotonin, another neurotransmitter that has deep calming and mood-boosting effects on the mind and body, is enhanced when you practice breathing exercises, which reduces feelings of anxiety and increases relaxation.
  Harvard researcher Herbert Benson coined the term "the relaxation response" to describe the body's calm reaction to the practice of deep breathing. In his 1975 book, *The Relaxation Response*, Benson used

scientific research to prove that slow deep breathing could alter the body's stress response.

In another study, published in the journal *Emotion,* researchers from the University of California, San Francisco, found that teachers who were taught to focus on their breath while meditating were less depressed, anxious, and stressed than those who didn't receive the training.

- **Increase your sex drive.** Often called the "cuddle hormone," the neurotransmitter oxytocin is triggered by deep breathing exercises. This chemical increases your libido and your desire for intimacy, and also increases feelings of optimism, self-confidence, and a sense of trust with others.

- **Reduce pain.** Full, slow, deep breathing stimulates the release of endorphins, which act as a natural pain reliever. Deep breathing with a meditative focus can also soothe the brain's circuits involved in sending signals of acute pain, like a headache or back pain, which can help lessen your perception of it.

   Slow deep breathing in conjunction with relaxing imagery is often recommended to those facing terminal illnesses and those in hospice care as a way to reduce discomfort and the need for analgesic drugs. The Lamaze method of conscious, patterned breathing stimulates relaxation and has helped many pregnant women cope with the pain of childbirth.

- **Improve concentration, clarity, and focus.** Deep, slow breathing increases blood flow to your prefrontal cortex and improves cognitive clarity and mental focus. It also improves concentration, alertness, and memory. The improved circulation that deep breathing offers also increases levels of creativity.

- **Encourage more complex brains.** Researchers at the University of California, Los Angeles, found that long-term meditators who were taught to breathe consciously and focus on the breath as part of a daily practice had more folds in their brains' cortexes in areas that are involved in emotional awareness, attention, self-recognition, and decision making, as compared to nonmeditators. These effects increased with how many years a person practiced, meaning that the longer you focus on your breathing, the smarter you will be.

- **Improve memory.** In a Harvard University study, researchers found that, with only eight weeks of training in breathing-focused meditation, meditators showed more growth in the areas of the brain associated with memory, as compared to the control group, who weren't taught better breathing techniques. The group who practiced better breathing also experienced decreased anxiety and an enhanced sense of calm and empathy toward others.

Your Breath and Your Body

Deep breathing offers a host of benefits for the body, including improving circulation, increasing lung capacity, lowering your heart rate, improving sleep quality, reducing asthmatic symptoms, and even reducing the risk of diabetes and some cancers. By balancing stress hormones with anabolic hormones, breathing right even helps you lose weight.

- **Improve immune function.** In a recent study, a team of researchers from the Netherlands found that people could enhance their body's immune response by controlling their breathing. The researchers split 24 volunteers into two groups: one group was the control, while the other underwent a training program designed by Dutch daredevil Wim Hof, which included meditation, breathing exercises, and ice-cold exposure. Both groups were then injected with a flu-like toxin to see the immune effects. (I'm glad I wasn't part of this study!) Those who underwent the training program and learned the breath-work reported fewer flu-like symptoms and showed lower indicators of inflammation and higher levels of an inflammation-fighting protein.

- **Reduce blood pressure.** When you take a long, full breath and then exhale fully and completely, your blood pressure naturally drops. When you slow and deepen your breathing, it triggers relaxation by activating the parasympathetic system and your vagus nerve. This nerve, which runs from your gut to your brain stem, inhibits the stress hormone cortisol and sends out the all-clear signal to tell your body that everything is okay.

- **Decrease asthma symptoms.** In a study published in the journal *Thorax*, Australian researchers found that when asthmatics performed breathing exercises, they reduced the needs for their rescue inhalers by 86 percent and dropped their use of inhaled corticosteroids by 50 percent, compared to those who didn't do breath work. It seems like most breathing exercises are helpful in easing asthma symptoms, as long as they are focused on deepening, slowing, and smoothing the breath. The most important aspect of a breathing technique for asthmatics is that it's one that is practiced regularly. Personally, I suggest following the recommendations for belly breathing on page 82 in this chapter. Studies have found that this technique can also help people who suffer from chronic obstructive pulmonary disease (COPD).

- **Sleep better.** If you've ever snuggled down in bed only to remain wide awake as your mind churned over a problem, then you know how racing thoughts can rob you of your sleep. Focusing attention on your breath, consciously slowing your breath, and shutting out distracting or running thoughts can all work together to help you fall asleep faster and sleep more restfully throughout the night.

  In a study published in *JAMA Internal Medicine*, researchers found that those who learned breathing-focused meditation slept better than those who received just a short education class on improving sleep habits. After just six weeks, the focused breathers reported less daytime fatigue and depression than the general education group.

- **Lose weight.** Okay—stay with me here. You know that better breathing lowers stress, and that stress makes you more likely to overeat or engage in emotional eating. In my book *Stubborn Fat Gone*™, I discuss how the stress hormone cortisol increases insulin levels, drops blood sugar levels, and increases our cravings for sugary, fatty foods. So making the link between better breathing and weight loss isn't that big of a leap.

- **Lower risk for chronic disease.** When you lower your level of oxidative stress, you lower the number of free radicals in your cells, which lowers your risk of chronic disease. In a study published in the journal *Evidence-Based Complementary and Alternative Medicine*, Italian researchers from the University of Camerino monitored 16 athletes while they did an intense workout. After the exercise, the athletes were divided randomly into two equal groups, and for 60 minutes, one group practiced diaphragmatic breathing (see page 82) while the other group just sat and rested with no instruction. The researchers found reduced levels of oxidative stress in the athletes who practiced the deep breathing techniques.

- **Look younger.** Research suggests that breathing-focused meditation can lower your levels of cortisol, a stress hormone that can cause you to age faster than you should. A daily session of deep breathing can induce a relaxed state, clear your mind, and keep you calm so you can keep the furrow between your brows relaxed. And, as we just learned, breathing techniques help reduce oxidative damage in your cells, which is another thing that leads to wrinkles! So save money on Botox—just breathe.

- **Improve digestion.** Diaphragmatic breathing (see page 82) can help release tension in your abdominal muscles, including your stomach, and ease indigestion. In a study published in the *American Journal of Gastroenterology*, researchers found that participants who learned breathing techniques to strengthen the diaphragm experienced less reflux over time than those who didn't get the training. When you practice bringing your attention and awareness to your breathing and begin to control your rate of breathing (specifically slowing down each inhale and exhale), you fully engage your diaphragm and relax your autonomic nervous system, which taps into your digestive system and helps it work more effectively.

What Better Breathing Does for Your Life

We've now gone over the research that shows the many benefits that better breathing can bring to your body and brain. Based on the research I've covered so far, below are all the potential ways that better breathing can help your life:

- **More loving relationships.** You'll be calm and happy, less easily riled, less likely to take offense, and less prone to conflict. You'll also regularly feel higher levels of empathy for your fellow man (and woman).

- **Better communication.** With your better sense of clarity and focus, along with an increased sense of confidence and relaxation, you'll be a better communicator. Of course, this will help both your personal and professional relationships.

- **Better work performance.** You'll be more focused and less distracted. You'll have more energy and you'll be more playful. With a boosted immune system, you'll take fewer sick days and be a more reliable employee.

TRY THIS: Sit Up Straight and Breathe Better

Slump over and really exaggerate poor posture. Let your neck drop forward, collapse your chest, and look down at your belly button. (You know, the kind of slouch your mother would shriek, "Stand up straight," about.) Now breathe as deeply as you can while in this position. Take a few breaths like this.

Okay?

Now sit up straight. Chest lifted, looking straight ahead. Now inhale deeply and exhale. Do this a few times.

Feel the difference? When you are slumped over, you compress your entire breathing apparatus. Your ribs don't have room to move, so your lungs can't expand fully, and your diaphragm muscle is also restricted. This all leads to trouble with breathing and can cause shortness of breath.

Now you know. One of the easiest fixes for better breathing has nothing to do with breathing at all. If you sit up straight you put your breathing equipment in the right position to provide you with the air you need. So stand tall and proud. :)

Better Breathing Techniques

"If you know the art of breathing you will have the strength, wisdom, and courage of ten tigers."

— Chinese proverb

Now let's focus on the "how" of breathing. In order to breathe better, you need to understand how to use the full capacity of your breathing apparatus—your nose, mouth, lungs, and diaphragm—to get the biggest benefits from the whole inhale/exhale cycle.

Your mouth and nose bring air to your lungs, where oxygen is extracted and passed into the bloodstream. This oxygenated blood is then taken to the tissues, organs, and cells that rely on it. Each day you breathe about 20,000 times, taking in an average of 2,100 to 2,400 gallons of air to meet your body's requirements. As you inhale, you absorb oxygen into your bloodstream for energy, and as you exhale, you excrete carbon dioxide as waste.

I've always found it fascinating that plants need the carbon dioxide we breathe out as waste, and we need the oxygen that plants excrete. If you think about it this way, then you can see how breathing in and out most fully benefits not only our own bodies, but also the earth in general.

Most people don't get the benefits they could from using the full range of their lungs and diaphragm to breathe in and out correctly, or, worse, they breathe in a way that exacerbates stress and anxiety instead of relieving it. According to anxiety and breathing expert

Joel McPherson, the average person uses only 20 percent of their lung capacity. However, with practice, you can learn how to tap into the full potential of your lungs.

It's important to focus on exhaling completely because stale air can build up in your lungs and leave less room for your diaphragm, which is actually the muscle responsible for doing about 80 percent of the work to fill your lungs. When stale air builds up, the diaphragm can't work to its full capacity, so the body starts to use other muscles in the neck, back, and chest for breathing—this can lead to neck and back pain and tension. This stale air is also the cause for reduced diaphragm function and muscle tension, so it's important that it doesn't build up. Focusing on diaphragmatic breathing and pursed-lip breathing can help you regain full use of your lungs. You'll find these exercises, as well as several other useful breathing techniques, outlined on the following pages. But first take the time to be mindful of how you are currently breathing.

Assess Your Own Breathing

When you breathe with your full lung capacity, your diaphragm and abdominal muscles pull on your abdominal cavity. This causes your chest to expand minimally, if at all, while your stomach expands significantly. So you can see how well you are using your lung capacity with the following simple test from Joel McPherson and the American Holistic Health Association (AHHA):

- Sit comfortably.
- Place one hand on your stomach and one on your chest.
- Breathe normally and pay attention to whether your stomach hand rises or your chest hand rises.

If your chest rises more than your stomach, you are not using your full capacity.

Now reflect on your general experience of your breathing. Do you feel like your breathing is often shallow? Are you often out of breath? Do you feel like your breathing is labored or too fast? If you are concerned about breathing, constricted feelings, or shortness of breath, make a call to your doctor today to set up further testing.

Please note that all exercises and tests in this chapter are in regard to normal breathing within safe parameters. You should contact a medical professional, call 911, or go to your local emergency room if you experience any of the following:

- Difficulty breathing that comes on suddenly and interferes with normal breathing

- Chest pain or pressure with shallow breathing or with breathing difficulty

- Difficulty breathing, can't catch breath after only slight activity

- Shortness of breath that wakes you up at night

- Tightness in throat or barking, croupy cough

High-Tech Breathing

You're just an app away from better breathing! My staff and I road tested several breathing apps. Here's what came out on top.

Breathe: Breathe is installed by default in Apple Watch OS 3. While developing the app, Apple tested it among hundreds of employees and a group of psychology and mindfulness experts. The app prompts you to focus on breathing for one minute every four hours, though you can change the time and frequency to suit your personal preferences. As you start your sessions, a blue-green mandala emerges and expands and contracts with your breath. (Cool, right?) If you want to close your eyes, the watch also gives you haptic feedback in the form of taps to prompt you when to inhale and exhale. After you finish, your recorded heart rate during the session is shown along with how many breathing sessions you have completed that day. This is by far my favorite app!

Calm: Designed to bring you more clarity, joy, and peace of mind, this application focuses on meditation. There are three different meditation programs you can choose from, and they even have one to help you sleep better! Filled with relaxing sounds and scenes, this is a great resource to a happier mind. It's available to download for free within Apple's App Store as well as Google Play.

Breathing Zone: This application promises to change our lives one breath at a time by focusing on mindful breathing exercises. With easy-to-follow voice instructions and an intuitive animated breathing guide, this app makes breathing even easier. (Not to mention, it's great for those of us who are visual learners.) The app features a detailed breathing guide and measures your breathing rate with an installed Breathing Analyzer. This app is also available on Apple's App Store and Google Play.

The Mother of All Breathing Exercises: Belly Breathing (AKA Diaphragmatic Breathing, or 4-7-8 Breathing)

This basic breathing technique can be used to benefit your brain, body, and soul in just about each and every way. I encourage you to try this exercise now and practice as often as possible. Work your way up to naturally breathing like this throughout the day.

This breathing technique is a foundational exercise that will help you improve sleep, reduce stress, release toxins, lower your blood pressure, reduce your heart rate, release feel-good hormones and neurotransmitters, improve your memory and focus, reduce pain, and improve your energy, circulation, and digestion.

The following steps are from Joel McPherson and the AHHA. You can also watch an online video titled "How to Perform the 4-7-8 Breathing Exercise" posted on YouTube by Andrew Weil, MD, where he teaches this technique (https://youtu.be/YRPh_GaiL8s). For a great, animated, kid-friendly video, check out the YouTube video "4-7-8 Breathing Exercise by GoZen," posted by GoZen! Anxiety Relief for Children (https://youtu.be/Uxbdx-SeOOo).

- **Inhale.** Begin by slowly breathing in through your nose, focusing on inhaling the air into your belly, not your chest, for a count of four. (You can put a hand on your stomach to see how well you're doing.)

- **Hold** your breath for a count of seven.

- **Exhale.** Slowly exhale through your mouth for a count of eight. As you exhale, try to make a soft whooshing noise by holding the tip of your tongue to the roof of your mouth.

- **Repeat** this process, called 4-7-8 breathing, three more times, for a total of four cycles. With practice you can work your way up to eight cycles, or breaths, at a time.

- **Progressions.** Start by doing this exercise two times per day, but be sure to stop if you become dizzy. As you increase your capabilities, add to your number of sessions until you can do four to eight breaths per hour all throughout your day.

Boost Breathing

If you are experiencing high anxiety and you only have a minute or so to calm down, you can try the following fun and easy breathing exercise. It was recently shared by one of my good friends, personal change expert Jairek Robbins, on one of my shows, Tiny Talks, on Facebook Live. (You can view these videos at Facebook.com/jorgecruise.)

- **Assess.** Rate your current stress level from 0 to 10, with 0 being no stress and 10 being really high stress.

- **Imagine** you're holding a bouquet of your favorite flowers right in front of your nose. (Alternatively, you can imagine a really expensive glass of wine or a bottle of your favorite scent.)

- **Breathe** deeply through your nose, imagining you're sniffing in this fabulous smell.

- **Breathe** in a bit more just when you think you've reached full capacity.

- **Hold** it for a few seconds.

- **Exhale** through your mouth while slumping forward slightly and dropping your head and shoulders.

- **Repeat** this three to five times total.

- **Reassess** your stress level now. (I bet it will be lower!)

Feel free to do this breathing technique as often as needed—whenever you feel like you need quick dose of calm energy. I find this technique especially helpful to do when dealing with difficult situations at work or in any public place. When you feel like you can't calm down and your heart is racing, this will provide the instant relief you need to lower stress.

Breath of Fire: Pump Up Your Mental and Physical Energy

If you are feeling sleepy or lazy and want to wake up caffeine-free, if you feel stuck in a mental fog, or if you are trying to get revved up for a workout, a technique that incorporates breathing more rapidly can help. Try the following exercise to feel instantly invigorated:

- **Inhale** from your belly and exhale through your nose.

- **Do it fast.** Continue to breathe in quick bursts, keeping your mouth closed but relaxed. Your breaths in and out should be equal in duration, but as short as possible. Aim for three in-and-out breath cycles per second, which will produce a lot of noise through your nose and quick movement of your diaphragm, like a bellows. (Setting a stopwatch while you do this is helpful.)

- **Breathe normally after each cycle.**

- **Start with 15 seconds.** Do not do this exercise for more than 15 seconds on your first try. Each time you practice, you can increase your time by five seconds or so, until you reach a full minute.

After this exercise, you'll likely feel invigorated, comparable to the heightened awareness you feel after a good workout. You should feel the effort at the back of the neck, the diaphragm (your belly area), the chest, and the abdomen. Feel free to do this breathing technique as often as needed. I find this technique is the perfect way to start off my morning because it gives a really great jolt of energy.

Breathing to Build Intimacy

This breathing technique comes to you courtesy of relationship coach Jordan Gray. You'll need an intimate partner with whom to practice; it's a perfect way to build connection, tenderness, and passion.

- **Get into position.** You can sit face-to-face or lie on your sides facing each other. Gently touch your foreheads together. Tilt your chins down so your noses aren't smooshed together, and look into each other's eyes.

- **Sync breaths.** Continuing to keep your foreheads connected, inhale slowly and deeply through your noses. Keeping time to your partner's inhale, pause at the top, and then exhale slowly and completely through your mouths.

- **Repeat for 7 to 15 breaths,** keeping time with your partner's breathing.

Feel free to do this breathing technique as often as you like, whenever you want to strengthen your emotional and physical connection with your partner.

Immune Booster: Using Breathing to Boost Your Immune Response

This is my interpretation of the Wim Hof method, which I referred to earlier in this chapter. It was developed by Wim Hof, a Dutch daredevil who is able to withstand extremely cold temperatures due to his breathing and meditative techniques. The following exercise will give you an incredible immune boost.

- **Warm up.** Sit comfortably in a chair, or cross-legged on the floor. Close your eyes. Take three slow deep breaths, in and out, focusing on releasing any tension in your body. On your fourth breath, inhale as deeply as you can through your nose, drawing your breath in until you feel a slight pressure from inside your chest. Hold for a moment, and then exhale completely through your mouth. (Imagine you are blowing out a candle, and suck your stomach in.) Hold at the bottom of your exhale for a moment. Repeat for a total of 15 warm-up breaths.

- **Balloon breathe.** Keeping your eyes closed, inhale deeply through your nose, and expand your belly fully. Next, exhale in a powerful burst through your mouth as if you were blowing up a balloon, drawing your belly button in toward your spine. Repeat for a total of 30 breaths, keeping a steady pace and focusing on using your belly to expand and contract with each inhale and exhale. Scan your body for any tension and focus on relaxing deeply. Because this portion will saturate your body with oxygen, you may experience light-headedness, tingling sensations, and surges of energy.

- **Breathe and hold.** Alternate between steps A and B below until you have done a total of six each.

    a. **Exhale and hold.** Inhale deeply through your nose as much as you can, and then blow out all the air until you've sucked your belly all the way in. Hold for as long as you can; start your next inhale when you can't hold your breath anymore.

    b. **Inhale and hold.** Inhale through your nose as much as you can, and hold your breath at the top for as long as you can, then exhale. Work your way up to a hold of 15 seconds. (Remember to alternate between steps A and B until you've done six of each.)

- **Relax for five minutes.** Return to regular breathing, and just keep your attention on your inhalations and exhalations. There is no need to exert any conscious control—just relax.

Feel free to do this breathing technique as often as needed, especially when you feel like you are getting sick or have inflammation. I especially recommend doing it during flu and allergy seasons to protect the immune system.

Breathing for Asthma and Anger: Breathing to Cool Hot Emotions

When you are feeling hot under the collar, agitated, frustrated, or angry, the common recommendation is to take a deep breath—but this is not the best advice. Neither is it recommended for someone suffering inflammation symptoms from asthma. Breathing deeply while in a stressed or agitated state can actually exacerbate your emotions by bringing more energy to them. This is because people who are in an agitated state will often start breathing more rapidly, even hyperventilating, when they try to breathe deeply. Rapid deep breathing is counterproductive because it can cut off oxygen to the brain and exacerbate panic attacks, anxiety, and mood swings. The advice for anger or asthma—two "hot" and inflamed states of being—should be to breathe more deeply and *slowly*.

The following exercises are great slow breathing techniques to use to settle down when you are feeling wound up either physically or mentally. They are even helpful for indigestion!

Slow Diaphragmatic Breathing

This is a variation on the main breathing exercise given on page 82. Whereas that technique is best used for everyday breathing, this technique is best used when you need to calm down and let your emotions cool off. Practice it any time you feel angry or feel your heart racing too fast.

The focus with this technique is slowing your breathing rate down, which will slow your heart rate and lower your blood pressure. You can also practice this while reclining in your bed, before going to sleep. This will also help you focus on contracting the diaphragm. When you exhale, try to only expand your belly, while not letting your chest rise. If you notice your chest rising or falling with your breath, put one hand on your chest and one on your belly. Then focus on the belly rising with each inhale and falling with each exhale.

This type of breath work can be used any time you feel emotionally triggered with feelings of anger, stress, or fear because it starts your body's relaxation response. The relaxation response, which is the opposite of the fight-or-flight stress response, helps your body to heal, repair, and renew.

- **Sit or lie comfortably.** Close your eyes and breathe naturally. Inhale through your nose and exhale through your mouth, bringing your attention to any areas of tension in your body and allowing them to relax.

- **Release all tension.** Feel the tension around and between your eyes melt away. Let your shoulders drop, soften your belly, feel your legs relax, unclench your hands.

- **Inhale and exhale slowly.** After you've scanned your body, on your next inhale focus on bringing in air through your nose slowly. Remember to breathe into your belly, not your chest. Count, "one, one-thousand, two, one-thousand," all the way up to 10, then pause for one moment.

- **Slowly exhale through your mouth.** Feel your belly deflate as you exhale and slowly count "one, one-thousand, two, one-thousand," to a count of 10.

- **Continue breathing in this way until you feel calm.** Focus on making each inhalation and exhalation slow, smooth, and steady for an equal count of 10 on each inhale and exhale. If you notice that your mind has wandered back to whatever had you wound up, anxious, or angry, gently bring your attention back to your breath.

Pursed-Lip Breathing

This exercise increases the amount of air you can take in and exhale, while also reducing the number of breaths you take each minute. It helps you be more physically active because it strengthens your lungs. I recommend practicing it two times a day, three days a week, particularly if you have any difficulty during a strenuous activity such as bending, lifting, or stair climbing.

This technique can also reduce stress and calm you down. This exercise is particularly beneficial to those who suffer from COPD and asthma because it helps purge stale air from your lungs and bring in more fresh air to nourish your body.

To do pursed-lip breathing:

- **Sit up straight and relax.** Feel the tension ease from your neck and shoulders, allow it to melt from your eyes and forehead, and let your belly soften.

- **Inhale through your nose to a slow count of five.** Breathe into your belly, not your chest. Count "one, one-thousand, two, one-thousand," all the way up to five, then pause for one moment.

- **Exhale slowly and completely for a count of 10.** Exhale through your mouth, with pursed lips, as if you are blowing out a candle.

- **Continue this pattern of inhaling and exhaling 5 to 10 times.** Focus on making each exhale twice as long as your inhale.

Pure Breath Exercise

This method is adapted from the Sangha Yoga teacher training manual and is designed to produce a calm breath and a calm mind. This exercise has many benefits if practiced regularly. I recommend starting off doing this exercise three times per day with 10 to 15 breaths, and then working your way up to 20 or 25 breaths each session, two times per week.

- **Sit comfortably.** Begin by sitting comfortably in a chair with both feet on the floor, or sitting on the floor with your legs crossed.

- **Pay attention.** Inhale and exhale three times. Bring your attention to your breath, listening and feeling your inhales and exhales without exerting any control or change to your breathing. Your aim is to just feel the sensation of inhaling and exhaling.

- **Slow down.** On your fourth inhalation, begin to slow your breath. Count the number of seconds as you inhale, "one-one thousand, two-one thousand," and so on, until you reach full capacity. Pause, then count as you exhale, and try to match your exhale to your inhale second for second.

- **Breathe even more slowly.** Continue to slow your breath even more while you listen and feel the sensation of each inhale and exhale. Smooth the transitions between each inhale and exhale, and the next inhale. Imagine your breath riding up as you inhale, like the car on a Ferris wheel circling up. When you reach the top, exhale and ride your breath down the Ferris wheel.

TRY THIS: Pair Affirmations with Your Breath

I love affirmations, and whenever I practice a breathing exercise I like to pair each inhale and exhale with an affirmation. Consider pairing any of the breathing exercises in this chapter with the affirmations you developed in the last chapter to support you in being imperfectly you and connecting with the feelings you really want to experience. The following are some of my favorites.

To practice with any of the relaxing breathing exercises:
"I believe in and accept myself just as I am in this moment."
"I feel radiant, relaxed, and full of light."
"I go within and ask what my soul needs today."
"I love the freedom I feel from releasing my thoughts."
"I inhale the light; I exhale the dark."
"Forgiving others frees me."
"I celebrate my beauty."

To practice with the Breath of Fire:
"I focus on my breath and I become relaxed and energized."
"Everyone I meet is refreshed by my positive energy and drive."
"I am strong and able."
"Today I fly."
"Every cell in my being is filled with energy and light."
"I am blessed with an endless supply of energy."
"My being is vibrant and glowing."

Your Rx:
Everyday Breathing

*"Breath is the power behind all things. I breathe in and
know that good things will happen."*

— Tao Porchon-Lynch

Breathing is something you do unconsciously all day. But now
I'd like you to consciously and mindfully practice the art of breathing. Once you experience the immediate benefits from these techniques, you will understand how powerful breath can be for your life.
To that end, I'd like you to get in the habit of doing breath work each
morning. But that's just the beginning! Make it a habit to consciously
practice better breathing in each of the following situations.

- **When you wake up.** Before getting out of bed, put
  one hand on your belly and one on your chest and
  focus on taking a few relaxing inhales through your
  nose and exhales through your mouth. You can keep
  your eyes closed as you focus on drawing air into
  your belly and exhaling air out of your belly.

- **While sitting at a stoplight.** This is the perfect
  opportunity to let go of any stress or tension that's
  been building in the day. In fact, it's become an
  automatic habit for me to start taking slow, deep
  breaths as soon as I see a red light. I've found that
  I can usually take about three or four deep, slow

inhales and exhales during this time—but you do need to keep your eyes open. (If you miss the light changing to green, the driver behind you will honk and you'll get instantly restressed!) Alternatively, if you are feeling sluggish or sleepy, this is a good time to do the breath of fire (see page 85).

- **If you feel out of balance.** Any time you feel overwhelmed, agitated, stressed, fearful, angry, sad, resistant—any time you feel triggered, hooked, or disturbed—choose one of the three exercises in "Breathing to Cool Hot Emotions" (see pages 88 to 91). Remember, the aim of slow deep breathing isn't about tamping down or stuffing feelings; it's about accepting your feelings—feeling your feelings, and investigating in a nonjudgmental manner.

- **If you feel asthma symptoms.** Remember that the same exercises that help with angry or hot emotions will help with asthma symptoms. Turn back to "Breathing for Asthma or Anger" (see page 88), and choose one of the three exercises.

- **Before a big meeting, job interview, or date.** If you are feeling tense before an appointment, meeting, or date, take a few minutes to practice some relaxing breathing. Refer back to the last section to choose what would make you feel better.

- **When you need a jolt of energy.** The breath of fire (see page 85) will rev you up whenever you feel that afternoon slump hitting—and it's calorie- and caffeine-free.

- **When you end your day.** For a more restful night's sleep, practice one of the relaxing breathing exercises for 5 to 10 minutes before you go to bed.

How to Start: Your 4-Week Practice

I'd like you to set aside a time for better breathing each day. Morning works the best for most people, but choose a time where you can set aside five minutes to start.

Week 1: 5 Minutes. Go back to the last section and choose a breathing exercise. If you have no preference, do the Mother of All Breathing Exercises. Make sure you are in an area where you won't be disturbed and do the exercise for five minutes every day this week.

Week 2: 10 Minutes. Double your time! Set your timer for 10 minutes and follow the same guidelines above. Do your chosen exercise every day this week.

Week 3: 15 Minutes. Again, sit or lie down in a quiet area and choose a breathing exercise that you can practice undisturbed for the full 15 minutes. Make sure you do so every day this week.

Week 4: Two sessions. Now aim to add in a second session in the evening. You can go back to 10 minutes at a time for this week, and then work at getting to 15 minutes in the following week. You might even choose a different exercise for each session—it's up to you.

Congratulations! You have now learned how to tap into the life-giving force of your breath. You've accepted your imperfect self, embodied your best you, and discovered how to breathe your way into balance and embrace the power of now. Now it's time for action! So take a nice, relaxing breath and choose to turn the page . . .

CHOICE 3
Move to Improve

*"Exercise is the most potent
yet underutilized antidepressant."*

— Bill Phillips

The third simple choice is to move to improve. For years as a celebrity fitness trainer, I always knew that movement was incredibly powerful to improve one's life. I myself have overcome my own weight issues because of movement. I've also seen many clients of mine completely change their lives and drop hundreds of pounds just by moving more!

But the latest breakthroughs in exercise science have shown that movement has many more benefits other than just physical ones. Your own movement controls your state of happiness more *quickly* than anything else. It is critical that you know that movement is probably the easiest tool to repeat again and again to instantly change your mood. I know I'm making it sound too easy, but we as humans are designed to move. We have legs, feet, hands, and fingers for a reason; we might as well use them to our benefit.

Practicing movement helps improve our physical and emotional health and well-being. I'm not prescribing you to become a CrossFit-loving, paleo Spartan warrior. But I am encouraging you to simply *move more*. I promise, if you just went for a walk, a bike ride around the neighborhood, or just straight-up danced your pants off in your living room, you'd feel the same mood-boosting effects as running five miles. It's the process that matters—not the outcome.

But first let's define what movement really is.

Movement is the opposite of static, not sitting still. Vibrating, fidgeting, pacing, dancing, walking, hiking, running, stretching, swimming, skiing, snowboarding, biking, playing racquetball, golfing, surfing, even getting out of your bed and shuffling to the kitchen to make a cup of coffee—all of these are examples of moving. From the simplest activities, like taking the dog for a walk around the block, to intense feats of strength, such as doing triathlons, all are forms of being active, and they all result in benefits.

Some sorts of activity serve you better than others—this is dependent on your personality, needs, preferences, and time constraints. Our focus here will be on using movement to magnify your mood, attitude, and actions in positive and empowering ways that will spur you to live the life you've always wanted.

By the end of this chapter, you will understand the new science on movement and know how you can effectively bring calm and clarity into your own life. You will also learn how movement can impact mood, health, and overall well-being.

So here's an overview of what's to come on the upcoming pages.

- *Why movement is essential.* Here you'll go on a discovery path to find the reasons why movement is essential to your life. I'll give you an overview of all the ways movement benefits your body, mind, and soul, including how it will flood your body with serotonin, your body's happy hormone.

- *Find your motivation.* In this section, I'll teach you the two types of motivation that push us to be our best selves and how to harness the power of personal meaning.

- *Find your routine.* Here I'll discuss a variety of methods through which you can incorporate more movement into your life and make it a habit.

- *Your Rx: Everyday moving.* In this section, we'll discuss how you can incorporate fun movement into your everyday life.

First, let me tell you how movement changed my life and became my ethos.

Why Movement Is Essential

"The first wealth is health."

— Ralph Waldo Emerson

Motivated by my own struggles with weight, I found the magic of movement back in my late teens. (I grew up in a Latin household where food was love, and, boy, did I love nachos.) My father's diagnosis of prostate cancer was what triggered it for me. From that moment on, health became a priority. I remember hearing a friend say to my father, "Your greatest wealth is health." This saying resonate and empowered me. Suddenly, something clicked. I wanted to be wealthy, not in finances but in my health.

I started attending a holistic medical practice with my father to learn the ins and outs of nutrition. Quickly after that, I joined a gym and started working out. To be honest, I wasn't quite sure what to do, so I just mimicked what others were doing around me. The main motivation for improving my health was to continue motivating my father to improve his, and I'm happy to say that my father made a full recovery. (He's still alive and kicking, by the way!)

In fact, my father and I *both* got fit and lost our excess weight, but there was so much more going on. Suddenly, I had the energy and desire to eat healthier foods, I felt more connected to people around me, and I noticed how much happier and less stressed I felt. On busy days that I couldn't go to the gym, I exercised at home with simple movements.

I knew that I'd discovered a little bit of magic with my quick at-home exercises. Indeed, they became the inspiration behind my first best-selling book *8 Minutes in the Morning*—quick and easy-to-do exercises that give you results. Little did I know then that spreading the message of health and fitness would become my life's mission. After the success of my first book, I saw the impact I was making on millions of lives and decided it was up to me to make the world a healthier place. Today, I am blessed to have helped millions of people learn the transformative effect of movement.

Movement is magical medicine. I know from firsthand experience that, no matter the ups and owns, a commitment to movement is an essential part of staying positive. In fact, I use movement to overcome stress and difficult situations. I can get stressed out with raising two sons, trying to meet my work deadlines, training celebrities, traveling . . . The list goes on, but I always make time to *move*. Walking is always my first preference, but when I can do more, I love all sorts of activities, from boxing to yoga. I know that if I don't move somehow, I feed into the negative thoughts that circle in my subconscious. Moving helps ease anxiety and stress and empowers the mind to think more clearly.

I know that you weren't buying an exercise book when you picked up *The 3 Choices*, so let me put that idea to rest right now. In this chapter, you'll learn the joy of being active, the thrill of moving your body and exercising for fun and well-being.

The type of movement we're going to talk about in this chapter will still provide all the benefits of a regular routine including the physical benefits: increasing your fitness, protecting your heart and lungs, lowering your risk of many types of cancers, decreasing your risk of diabetes, reducing the pain of arthritis, and helping you live longer. And then there are the mental and emotional effects: exercise triggers your brain to release a surge of feel-good chemicals (serotonin, dopamine, and endorphins) that boosts your mood, reduces stress, increases energy, eliminates doubt and fear, builds confidence, and empowers you to live fully and freely.

The Movement Effect

Have you ever noticed how you feel after an unusually active day? Maybe it was a day at the beach playing volleyball, or a family hike or bike ride, or perhaps you just got caught up last Sunday doing yard work—and while you might be tired and sore, I'll bet that you also have that good tired feeling that comes from exercise. You feel calm, settled, serene, energized, and happy. It's no illusion; exercise is as powerful as medicine in its effects on mood and physical health, according to a wealth of scientific research.

Your Brain on Exercise

- *A better mood.* Physical activity stimulates the release of all sorts of feel-good chemicals in your brain. Endorphins work to shut down negative thinking, while exercise's serotonin-boosting effects have been shown to reduce depression.

  In one Cochrane review, researchers ran a foundational meta-analysis of 23 studies looking at exercise and depression and concluded that exercise had a "large clinical impact" on depression. Other research published in the *Archives of Internal Medicine* found that exercise was as effective as Zoloft for those suffering from major depression.

- *Stress relieving.* Research shows that regularly participating in physical activity is empowering and confidence building, and some team sports— racquetball, soccer, tennis, and even kickboxing and aerobics—build a team, or herd, mentality and reduce anxiety and relieve stress. In one study (with what I consider to be questionable ethics), published in the *American Journal of Psychiatry*, researchers found that when they chemically induced anxiety in two groups of adults who suffered from anxiety disorders, those who had just finished exercising for 30 minutes were less likely to have a panic response to the injection than the group that had just rested.

- *Memory enhancing.* Got brain fog? Get moving, say University of British Columbia researchers. Their study, published in the *British Journal of Sports Medicine*, found that people who engage in regular heart-pumping, sweat-producing exercise had larger hippocampi, which is the area in your brain involved in memory and thinking. In other research, neurologists have found a link between moderate exercise and an increase in the volume of selected brain regions that are linked to better brain function.

- *A natural high.* You've probably heard of the "runner's high"; many people report that they feel a natural sense of euphoria after they exercise. In the past, research has pointed to the release of endorphins that trigger a response similar to opioid drugs. Recently, researchers in Germany discovered a different connection: the same area in the brain that is triggered to induce a high by the THC in marijuana also seems to be activated by exercise.

  The team of investigators had a group of mice that were used to running on an exercise wheel. They then split the mice into two groups and had half the mice remain sedentary and half run on the wheel for five hours. The exercising rodents were far less anxious and had a higher tolerance for pain than their slothful counterparts. In a second phase of the study, the researchers gave the mice a marijuana-blocking agent and tested the wheel-running mice again; this time they were just as anxious and felt as much pain as the slothful group, leading the investigators to believe that exercise triggers those receptors.

Your Body on Movement

Just about everyone knows that exercise improves health—just about every aspect of health. The research findings are so vast and have become such an accepted part of the medical literature that I'm just going to give you a quick rundown here of the most promising benefits:

- Lose weight
- Reduce heart disease
- Strengthen your lungs
- Breathe easier
- Lower blood pressure
- Decrease cancer risk
- Lessen arthritis pain
- Improve bone density
- Shed belly fat
- Boost your immune system
- Live longer

More than Exercise: Everyday Moving

Movement is about more than just exercise. In fact, you can do a lot to boost your health and your mood by just cutting out some of the time that you sit on your derriere.

NEAT (non-exercise activity thermogenesis) is the energy that your body expends in any activity that is not sleeping, eating, or formal exercising—in plain language, it's your everyday moving. This can include typing, tapping your toes, drumming your fingers, fidgeting, pacing, walking, doing yard work, folding laundry, and so on. According to Dr. James Levine, a professor of medicine at the

Mayo Clinic who founded the NEAT little acronym, you can make big changes with small movements. In fact, the benefits of NEAT don't seem to be linked to the intensity of the activity, but the frequency and duration.

In fact, the most powerful commitment you could make right now isn't to exercise more but simply to cut the time you spend on your sofa, at your desk, or in your car. According to a study by Dr. James Levine, who studies the effects of sedentary behaviors, women who sit for more than six hours a day have a 37 percent increased risk of early death as those who sit for less than three hours a day—and this is separate from how often the women exercised formally. For men, there was a 17 percent increased risk when comparing those who sit for more than six hours a day and those who sit for less than three hours a day. Exercise was found to lower, though not eliminate, the mortality risk tied to sitting. So get off your butt as often as you can, increase your NEAT, and get moving!

TRY THIS: Increase Your NEAT and Slash Your Sitting

Think about various strategies you can begin to weave into your daily routine to increase your activity and decrease your sitting time. Here are some suggestions:

- Take the stairs instead of using the elevator or escalator.

- Park far away from the grocery store or your office entrance.

- Walk or bike while doing your local errands.

- Wash your car by hand.

- Schedule walking dates instead of coffee dates.

- Get off one stop early from the trolley or bus.

- Stand up and do five minutes of activity for every hour you are seated—do anything! Turn on some of your favorite music, and just get up and boogie.

- Skip the drive-through; always get out and walk instead.

- If you must sit, then knit, crochet, put together a puzzle, play a game with the kids, fold laundry, or at least read—anything but watch TV. (You burn more calories even when sitting and meditating than you do watching a show on television.)

TRY THIS: The Anti-stress Remedy

As a nutrition specialist, I am always researching products to improve our lives, especially when it comes to stress. While I believe that movement is the best remedy for overcoming anxiety, I also want to share with you a product I've used for the past 15 years that helps me keep calm and carry on: Natural Calm by Natural Vitality.

Natural Calm is a fruity, sparkling supplement drink that promotes healthy magnesium levels and balances your calcium intake to help you feel less stressed and more relaxed. It features highly absorbable, water-soluble magnesium in ionic form, so it's ready to go to work in your body right away.

So what does magnesium have to do with stress? It turns out that most people don't get enough magnesium in their diets, yet ingest an excess amount of calcium (usually from dairy products). High calcium levels and stress-filled lives deplete the magnesium in the body, and this increases your feelings of stress and anxiety. Using a supplement like Natural Calm replenishes your body with proper levels of magnesium and balances your calcium levels to not only avoid stress upon your cells but also create a relaxed state. Furthermore, when it comes to supplementation with magnesium, the body takes what it needs and excretes any excess, so you can only benefit from trying Natural Calm.

I highly encourage you to give Natural Calm a try. It has completely changed the way my body reacts to stress and has helped me remain calm whenever life throws me a curveball. Head on over to www.naturalvitality.com to get some free samples sent to your door.

I've learned that reasons come first, reaching your goals comes second. So let's examine the reasons that motivate us.

Find Your Motivation

"Swimming is normal for me. I'm relaxed. I'm comfortable, and I know my surroundings. It's my home."

— Michael Phelps

Over the course of my life, I've helped millions of people move and lose the weight that had been holding them back for years. What I've found is that the key to motivating anyone to do anything is *reasons.* Because the meaning behind your goals is much more impactful than your goals themselves. You may want to be a doctor, but if you just want to be a doctor to please your parents, then I'm afraid your motivation won't be as high as someone who wants to find a cure for cancer. So it's important to put meaning behind your goals.

Harness the Power of Personal Meaning

My client Maria knew that exercise was good for her and something she *should* do, but she hated the gym. She despised going nowhere on a treadmill and found the weight machines mundane and mechanical. She could stick to the gym or aerobics classes for a month or so, but then she'd start skipping her workouts and fall back into a slump.

One day, as we were talking during a session, Maria was expressing her disdain for the fitness club. I asked her what she loved to do most of all, and she told me that she had grown up camping and hiking but hadn't done it for years. Maria shared that she had a special connection with her father, with whom she had backpacked and camped for many years. She was feeling a lot of grief, as he had died recently.

I helped Maria find some local hiking trails, and we met for our next session at one that was just a 10-minute drive from her house. The hike was challenging for Maria, but at the top of the mountain her cheeks were flushed and her eyes sparkled. "*This* is what I've been missing," she told me.

Today, Maria hikes that mountain most days of the week, and loves it so much that she gets up at 5 A.M. to get her hike in before her workday starts. "I feel a spiritual connection to my father, grand-parents, and to the world at large," Maria told me. She's used her reborn love of hiking to inspire trips with her family to Yosemite, the desert, and Sierras. Not only is she internally motivated to exercise, but also she is spreading the love to her family members.

Maria is just one example of a client finding what works for her. I have clients who are the exact opposite of Maria: they love the gym, love the atmosphere, and have a strong squad of fitness buddies. It's not the specific goal or method that matters, it's what you love and feel connected to that makes all the difference.

Finding Your Reasons to Move

Understanding the difference between extrinsic and intrinsic motivators is key to having a commitment to movement that will last. Extrinsic motivation comes from the external—your doctor or spouse telling you that you need to exercise, or a T. rex chasing you down. Intrinsic motivators are from your internal desire to feel better and learning to exercise for its own sake, as expressed by Michael Phelps in the quote that begins this section. A wealth of scientific research tells us that intrinsic motivation is the key to making movement a self-motivating and automatic habit in your life.

Last year, my friend Alex, who is executive producer for the *Steve Harvey Show*, asked me to do a weight-loss competition on the show where I would transform the lives of five co-workers from Chicago. The first day that I met the "Fabulous Five," as I called them, I sat them down and asked why they wanted to lose the weight. They immediately gave typical answers such as "to be healthy" and "to feel good." I then told them that in order to really lose the weight, they needed to dive deeper and discover what losing the weight truly meant to them.

I gave them an assignment to discover the top reasons that resonated with them about why they wanted to lose weight. To help them find their deeper meanings, I asked them to first write down the major problems they have with their life. Then I asked them to find the common denominator among all their problems, and then write down what they would want to do first if their problem went away.

- Alisha's desire was to have health that invigorated her instead of dragging her down, and to break into the acting world with confidence in her body.

- Emily's desire was to look beautiful on her wedding day and finally show the world who she always saw herself to be.

- Kaitlyn's desire was to be able to backpack through Europe without any struggles.

- Suresh's desire was to be able to provide for his family and not jeopardize his health and future.

- Jen's desire was to be able to have a child with her husband.

Once they were able to identify these core reasons, their commitment to nutrition and fitness became even stronger.

TRY THIS: Find Your Personal Motivation to Move

Reasons don't have to be long and complex, but they have to be authentic and meaningful to your core self. So are you ready to find your reason to move?

Write down the top three areas of your life that you want to improve. Think about what motivated the Fabulous Five and also consider common motivations, such as: How do you want to your body to look? What activities do you want to do on the weekends? How do you want your family/spouse/kids to think about you?

1.

2.

3.

I've found that a good night's sleep helps bring focus, so I want you to come back to this page tomorrow and circle the reason that resonates with you most—that is your reason to move.

Create Hardwired Habits

In this section, I'm going to teach you how to create intrinsic motivation through simple habit-forming behaviors: linking your cue to exercise (e.g., laying out exercise clothes) to your reward (e.g., how you feel when you are done with your spin class). I want you to feel like Phelps about your own movement choices. When you learn to make a choice personally rewarding and meaningful, it will become something you look forward to rather than something you avoid. But to create a new habit, you first need to know how the brain *works* when it is learning something new, and then how the brain *acts* when it is engaged in a learned behavior.

In *The Power of Habit*, Charles Duhigg, a Pulitzer Prize–winning writer for the *New York Times*, outlines how neurobiologists have discovered that when you learn a new activity, you engage your thoughtful, intentional, decision-making brain—your thinking brain. After you've had the time to repeatedly perform that activity, it becomes an established behavior (a habit), and your thinking brain can put its attention on other matters, and just let the instinctual, unconscious brain take over. In other words, a habit is an automatic behavior ruled by your unconscious brain—and just about anything can be made into a habit, whether good or bad.

The bad news is that you can't ever really lose a bad habit; they are always lurking in your brain, ready to be reactivated. The good news is that you can learn and activate healthy new habits. Then, over time, those new, better habits can deactivate the old, bad habits in the same way that you can turn up your headphones loud enough with your favorite tunes and drown out the lame music that's playing at the gym.

Researchers who study habit-forming behaviors say that up to 45 percent of our daily activities are made up of a series of habits. If we didn't have this ability, then we'd have to think consciously every time we do any little thing. Every time you got in your car, you would have to consciously think about how to put the key in the ignition, put the car into reverse, turn the steering wheel, and so on, paying attention to every detail and making conscious decisions at every turn. What happens instead is that you grab your coffee and get in the car, and the next thing you know you are pulling into your parking space at work. While you want to be conscious of what you are doing, being overly conscious would be exhausting. So habits save the day by saving your brain energy, which saves your willpower—to a point. Willpower is an exhaustible resource (it works better in the morning, when you are fresh, and wears out as the day goes on), which is why it is easier to eat healthy in the morning but give in to ice cream after dinner every night.

The brain has a tendency to overthink, which can work against you if you are trying to establish a new healthy habit. For example, you might say, "Maybe I should skip my training session because the road is too wet, it's too hot, I don't have the right clothes, I didn't download the right music, the time is too tight, it's too far . . ." and so on.

That's why you want to turn your movement routine into an automatic habit. When you choose activities that resonate with your personal meaning and allow them to become an instinctual habit, then you won't even have to think about it—you'll just end up being active often, being happy about it, and reaping all the benefits that come with regular activity.

Forming a habit can be broken down into three simple steps: the cue, the routine, and the reward. Duhigg calls this the "Habit Loop." The key here is that it is the cue and the reward that are the most important factors in making the exercise habit stick.

Here's the breakdown, adapted from Duhigg's book:

1. **The Cue.** This is the automatic trigger that starts the behavior—for the purposes of this chapter, this will be what you do at night to prepare for the next day's activity. Before you go to bed at night, you are going to lay out or pack whatever workout clothes, shoes, socks, and gadgets you'll need, and put everything right where you can see it or trip over it. This is your cue: just seeing the clothes and items you prepared and put in an obvious spot. Other cues can be a set date you have to go running with a group of friends, or a trio of friends you meet for a set racquetball date.

   My hiking client, Maria, sets out her hiking pants, sports bra, shirt, jacket, socks, hiking boots, headphones, car keys, and dog's leash every night. She also puts her driver's license in a zippered pocket, fills her bottle of water, folds up some tissues and puts them in her jacket pocket, and puts doggie bags in her other pocket. She sets all the items right by her bed, where she can see them. It's the attention to all the details that makes it easy for the conscious behavior to take a backseat. With the prework done, it is easy for Maria to just roll out of bed and practically fall into her workout clothes.

Since I often work out at the gym, I do the same thing, but I pack everything I need in my gym bag before I go to bed, and I put it at the front door with my keys on top. I lay out all the clothes I'll be wearing, including socks and shoes. Then I set my coffee to be ready as soon as my alarm goes off in the morning.

2. **The Routine.** As soon as you start to get dressed, or pick up your gym bag, or see your trio of friends for your set racquetball date, you are already beginning the routine—this is the behavior itself that you want to make into a habit. The first week that I had Maria do this, she reported back to me that it felt like an effort, but by the second week she found that just putting on her hiking pants clicked her into auto mode. (Did you get that? *Auto mode* is code for *routine*.)

When you set up a routine and then follow it for as little as one week, you engage the part of your brain that is the default and unconscious setting. This is powerful because once you have this start-up routine in place, it will become instinctual. Then the second part of your routine (the actual movement that you do) will fall into place. While variety is an important part of creating a long-term movement routine, it's important to start out with simple go-to movements that can become habitual.

3. **The Reward.** This is what helps your brain remember to do steps one and two. One German study that looked at this had exercisers use a small piece of chocolate as the reward. (Not my first choice, of course. I would have gone for some strawberries! But the piece of chocolate was tiny.) After six months, the researchers found that 58 percent of those people were more likely to be exercising, and they had

even stopped eating the chocolate. The endorphins, serotonin, and dopamine that were released by doing the exercise (the routine) had become a natural replacement for the chocolate (the reward).

The neurotransmitters released during exercise will reward you naturally for doing the exercise—but as you begin creating your habit loop, the reward is what may do the trick. Maybe your reward is a small piece of chocolate; indulging in a favorite Netflix series; or simply tracking your exercise as soon as you complete it with a phone app, Apple Watch, pedometer, or fitness tracker. Some people find that posting their exercise on social media is not only rewarding, but also holds them accountable. Whatever you choose, make sure that it's something that you can give yourself immediately after you have finished exercising, or something that automatically generates feedback.

In brain scans that look at the phenomenon of the habit loop, researchers find that this final phase is when the entire brain just clicks back into engagement. After the second week of consistent movement, you can start to phase out the reward, especially if it is caloric in nature. By this time, the intrinsic influence of those natural brain chemicals will start to be their own reward—as will the smaller numbers on the scales and the extra room in your jeans.

TRY THIS: Find Your Reward

What reward would motivate you to get moving? Here are some ideas:

- Buy the new workout clothes that you've always wanted.

- Create a workout playlist that you love listening to.

- Pamper yourself with a massage (especially if you get sore).

- Give yourself some "you time," even if it's just five minutes of scrolling through Facebook.

- Indulge in a healthy treat like chocolate covered bananas or frozen yogurt.

- Grab some fresh flowers from your florist and put them on display.

- Watch a television show or movie guilt-free.

- Treat yourself to a facial, manicure, or pedicure.

Bonus: Think of cues and rewards that would help you create habit loops for each of the three choices!

How do you want to get moving? The next section offers exercise ideas to help you with the "routine" part of your new movement habit loop. Whether you are a beginner or more advanced, I have all the exercises you'll need to move to improve. Remember, you should choose an exercise routine that fits the best with your life and schedule—whatever is reasonable for you to commit to.

Find Your Routine

"Reading is to the mind what exercise is to the body."

— Joseph Addison

This section includes exercises that fall under three levels of difficulty (some may seem easier or harder based on your experience). If you have been mostly sedentary (not exercising), start the activity of your choosing for just 10 to 15 minutes the first session, and then work up from there.

For most of the following exercises, I offer a sample schedule to help you start incorporating more exercise over the next few weeks. Whenever you engage in formal exercise, follow this three-phase format: a warm-up, which is just the chosen activity at an easy pace; the main activity at an intensity that feels moderately challenging; and then a cooldown, which is just the same activity at an easy pace. On an exertion scale of 1 to 10, with 0 being nothing at all (sitting in a chair) and 10 being the most extremely difficult exercise you can imagine (after an all-out sprint), this is what your exercise intensity should look:

Warm-up: 1 to 3 (light to moderate)

Main movement: 4 to 6 (moderately brisk to heavy or moderately hard)

High-intensity interval training: 7 to 9 (very difficult, all-out effort)

Cooldown: 3 to 1 (moderate to light)

Any one of these ways to exercise is great. From my experience, if you are choosing a workout from the easy category, you will feel good. When it's from the moderate category, you may feel better as you can get a bigger rush of endorphins. I personally get the biggest rush with the difficult activities; they keep my mood elevated and help me feel my best. As you try the more difficult workouts, you may feel that you get more of a rush of endorphins and feel even better as well.

Remember, the goal for any of the following activities is to start where you are and to *have fun*.

Easy Moving

Walking

This is a perfect beginner exercise. You can just lace up some good walking shoes and head out your front door.

Week 1: Warm up for the first 2 to 3 minutes, and then pick up your pace for 8 to 10 minutes, and then cool down for 2 to 3 minutes. Aim to get out walking three times this week.

Week 2: Warm up for 3 minutes, then pick up your pace to 10 to 15 minutes, and then cool down for 3 minutes.

Week 3: Warm up for the first 3 minutes, then pick up your pace to a brisk pace for 15 to 20 minutes, then cool down at an easy pace for 3 minutes.

Week 4: Warm up for 3 minutes, then pick up your pace to a moderately brisk pace for 20 to 25 minutes, then cool down for 3 minutes.

Subsequent Weeks: Continue to extend your time until you are doing 45 minutes of brisk walking for your main workout. You can keep your warm-up and cooldown the same. If time constraints don't allow you to extend your time, increase your difficulty by looking for routes that add in hills, or use a treadmill with inclines. If you feel ready, think about switching to a moderate-level activity.

Low-Impact Aerobics

Many gyms, fitness clubs, community centers, community colleges, and YMCAs offer low-impact aerobics classes, such as Zumba, general aerobics, Jazzercise, and step aerobics. You can check out water fitness classes for low-impact activity that is easy on your joints and offers strengthening benefits. Some of these classes are offered for those who know nothing about doing a crawl or the butterfly. Call around to your gym, health club, community center, or YMCA to see what is available.

For aerobics classes, make sure you have some good aerobic-style shoes. (Note that these are different from running or walking shoes, which are designed for forward motion; aerobics shoes are made for moving side to side and on the diagonal.) For swim classes, you'll need a swimsuit (of course), water shoes (optional, usually), and a fun attitude.

Week 1: Take one class this week and see how you like it. Do some walking two other days this week.

Week 2: Take two classes this week, whether it's the same from the previous week or a different one. Walk or take a low-impact aerobics class another day this week.

Week 3: Now you are ready to take three classes this week.

Week 4: Take four classes this week, but try to make one of them a more advanced class. Look into adult swimming lessons, or see if there is a land class you might enjoy.

Subsequent Weeks: To keep your motivation high, tap into your herd mentality. Get to know the names of at least three other people who go to the classes regularly with you. Do something together after class, for a social reward in your habit loop.

Moderate Moving

If you are comfortable completing at least 30 minutes a day of one of the Easy Moving activities, then you are ready to exercise at this level.

Hiking

Many people make the mistake of thinking that hiking is the same thing as walking—not so. The uneven terrain of hiking trails is very different from strolling, or even a fast walk down a street or sidewalk. Even if you walk regularly, you'll want to give yourself a little extra prep time for getting up to speed because hiking adds extra demands on your heart, lungs, muscles, and your balance.

First things first, invest in a pair of hiking shoes. If the terrain is really rough, consider getting a pair that provides extra ankle support. Take your time, and go for short distances at first. The cool thing about trail walking is that your body will be required to make constant minor adjustments to adapt to the ever-changing trail—that means more muscle and core building for your body, and more calories burned for you.

Weeks 1 and 2: Warm up for the first 2 to 3 minutes, pick up your pace for 8 to 10 minutes, and then cool down for 2 to 3 minutes. Aim to get out hiking one or two times this week.

Weeks 3 and 4: Warm up for 3 minutes, pick up your pace for 10 to 15 minutes, and then cool down for 3 minutes. Aim to get out hiking two to three times this week.

Weeks 5 and 6: Warm up for 3 minutes, pick up your pace for 15 to 20 minutes, and then cool down at an easy pace for 3 minutes. Aim to get out hiking three to four times this week.

Weeks 7 and 8: Warm up for 3 minutes, pick up your pace to a moderately brisk pace for 20 to 25 minutes, and then cool down for 3 minutes. Aim to get out hiking three to four times this week.

Subsequent Weeks: Continue to extend your time until you are doing 45 minutes of brisk hiking for your main workout. You can keep your warm-up and cooldown times the same. If time constraints don't allow you to hike for longer or more often, look for routes that add in more difficulty.

Jogging

This is the exercise for you if you want to ramp up your walking routine but aren't quite ready to start running a 5K, much less all 26.2 miles of a marathon. Jogging is easier than you think! You'll burn more calories in the same amount of time that you spend walking, you'll feel greater mood-boosting and stress-reducing results, and you'll get more bone-density-building benefits from this body-jostling exercise. If you're a beginner, I suggest that you spend at least six weeks with a walking routine before transitioning to jogging. This will give your body, muscles, tissues, and joints time to get accustomed to the new, bouncier you.

For both your warm-up and cooldown, consider doing three minutes of easy walking. I recommend jogging three times a week on nonconsecutive days (so either Monday, Wednesday, Friday; or Tuesday, Thursday, Saturday).

Week 1: Warm up, then pick up your walking pace and do 4 minutes of walking and 1 minute of easy jogging. Repeat this 4:1 sequence three more times for a 20-minute total, and then cool down for 3 minutes.

Week 2: Warm up. Do 3 minutes of fast walking and 2 minutes of jogging. Repeat this 3:2 sequence three more times for a 20-minute total, and then cool down for 3 minutes.

Week 3: Warm up. Do 3 minutes of fast walking, and 3 minutes of jogging. Repeat this 3:3 sequence three more times for a 24-minute total, and then cool down for 3 minutes.

Week 4: Warm up. Do 2 minutes of fast walking and 3 minutes of jogging. Repeat this 2:3 sequence three more times for a 20-minute total, and then cool down for 3 minutes.

Week 5: Warm up. Do 1 minute of fast walking and 4 minutes of jogging. Repeat this 1:4 sequence three more times for a 20-minute total, and then cool down for 3 minutes.

Week 6: Warm up. Do 1 minute of walking and five minutes of jogging. Repeat this 1:5 sequence three more times for a 24-minute total, and then cool down for 3 minutes.

Week 7: Warm up. Do 2 minutes of fast walking and 6 minutes of jogging. Repeat this 2:6 sequence three more times for a 32-minute total, and then cool down for 3 minutes.

Week 8: Warm up. Do 2 minutes of fast walking and 7 minutes of jogging. Repeat this 2:7 sequence two more times for a 27-minute total, and then cool down for 3 minutes.

Week 9: Warm up. Do 1 minute of fast walking and 8 minutes of jogging. Repeat this 1:8 sequence two more times for a 27-minute total, and then cool down for 3 minutes.

Week 10: Warm up. Do 1 minute of fast walking and 9 minutes of jogging. Repeat this 1:9 sequence two more times for a 30-minute total, and then cool down for 3 minutes.

Subsequent weeks: Phase out the 1 minute of walking, or keep it—and slowly inch up on your times until you can run for 45-minute sessions with minimal walk breaks. Always do jogging on nonconsecutive days to give your joints and bones a chance to rest.

Body-Weight Fitness

This is one of my favorite beginner strength-training routines. After warming up for 3 minutes with easy jogging or walking in place, do all of the following moves three times a week on non-consecutive days.

1. Waist Whittler (3 sets of 10 reps per side)

To start, get down on the floor on your hands and knees, and then move into a push-up position so that your body forms a straight line from your head to your heels. (If you have joint issues, feel free to modify the position by resting on your knees.) Look at the ground, but don't let your head sag, and keep your abdominal and back muscles tight. Slowly pull your left knee up so that it touches your left elbow, then return to your starting position. Next, pull your right knee up so that it touches your right elbow, then return to your starting position. Repeat, alternating sides. (For added difficulty, touch each knee to the *opposite* elbow, crisscrossing your body instead of remaining on the same side. This engages more muscle groups.)

2. Butt Buster (3 sets of 10 reps)

Start by lying on the floor on your back with your arms down along the sides of your torso. Bend your knees to slide your feet back until they are a couple of inches in front of your knees. Now tighten your butt muscles and pull your hips up, keeping your arms and feet flat on the ground. You should form a straight line from shoulders to knees. Slowly lower your hips to the floor. Repeat.

3. Shoulder Shaper (3 sets of 10 reps)

Sit on the floor with your knees bent and your feet flat on the floor in front of you, several inches in front of your knees. Place your hands on the floor a few inches behind your butt, fingertips pointing toward your backside. Make sure your arms are shoulder width apart. Pull your hips up from the floor while keeping your hands and feet flat on the floor, forming an upside-down tabletop position. Keep your elbows bent; you should be working out your arm muscles. Dip down to return to the floor, then repeat.

4. Chest Chiseler (3 sets of 10 reps)

Get down on the floor on your hands and knees, like a modified push-up position. Rather than keeping your hands under you, pull your hands close together and allow your fingers to touch at the thumbs and index fingers, forming a diamond shape. Slowly lower your chest to the floor, and then push yourself back up. Repeat. (If you are having a hard time doing this move, you can do it on a table or chair instead of the floor.)

5. Thigh Trimmer (3 sets of 10 reps per side)

Stand with your feet hip width apart and raise your hands out straight in front of you, shoulder width apart, palms facing the floor. Pull your left foot up in front of you, keeping it about six inches off the ground. Squat down by bending your right knee, being careful to maintain your balance, then raise yourself back to a neutral standing position. Switch sides, raising your right foot and squatting down on your left leg. Alternate sides; each raise and lower is one rep.

Challenging Moving

When you are ready for your most vigorous exercise challenges, move into this category. You can find samples of each of these workouts at jorgecruise.com.

- Sprinting
- Surfing
- Racquetball
- Kickboxing
- HIIT (high-intensity interval training)

HILO Yoga HIIT Workout

High-intensity interval training (HIIT) is a form of cardiovascular exercise that focuses on alternating short periods of intense exercises with less intense recovery periods. I find that it's the most efficient way to lose weight and build stamina. An HIIT workout can be created using any type of activity, such as swimming, running, weightlifting, or yoga. The following is a sample HIIT routine that I like to use, based on HILO yoga, a workout that I created a year ago. HILO stands for "high-intensity, low-intensity," and it combines recovery yoga poses with high-intensity exercises.

I strongly recommend that anyone who is able to do so incorporate an HIIT workout into their routine, whether it be HILO yoga or another activity. This should be doable for those in excellent health who can work out at a moderate pace. (Remember to always consult with your doctor when starting an exercise routine.) If you are a beginner, you can still do an HIIT routine. Just be sure to choose easier exercises, go a bit more slowly, and don't push yourself to do all the reps—you don't want to hurt yourself or overdo it.

Do HILO yoga or another HIIT workout three times a week on nonconsecutive days (Monday, Wednesday, Friday, or Tuesday, Thursday, and Saturday). Each workout consists of two cycles of four moves with a quick break between cycles as well as a warm-up before and a cooldown after. Here's how this sample workout should play out:

Warm Up
Cycle 1
Rest 30–60 seconds
Cycle 2
Rest 30–60 seconds
Cycle 1
Rest 30–60 seconds
Cycle 2
Rest 30–60 seconds
Cool Down

Warm-Up:

Walk in place, jog gently, circle your arms, lift and lower your shoulders, lift and lower your knees, or dance around—any sort of movement will do.

Cycle 1:

1. Torso Twist (15 reps per side)

Sit on the ground with your legs crossed under you, back upright with good posture. Put your hands behind your head with your elbows out and arms parallel to the ground. Twist your body at the waist so that you're looking to the right, allowing your arms to rotate to the right along with you. Return to your original position, then turn at the waist so you face the other way. Repeat these movements quickly, alternating sides.

2.   *Garland Pose (30 seconds)*

Stand tall with feet approximately shoulder-distance apart, toes pointed out, and palms pressed together in front of you. Sit down in a squat while balancing your weight on the back of your heels, feet flat on the ground. Your thighs should be slightly wider apart than your torso. Exhale as you lean your torso slightly forward between your thighs. Press your elbows against your inner knees while resisting your knees against your elbows. Hold this position for 30 seconds.

3. Shadow Boxing (15 reps per side)

Sit on the ground with your legs crossed under you, back upright with good posture. Raise your fists up in a boxing position, keeping your elbows in and pointing down. Keep your chest lifted as you quickly punch each arm straight in front of you, alternating sides. (For added difficulty, punch each fist across your body while rotating your torso.)

4. *Plank Hold (30 seconds)*

Start in a push-up position on the floor with your toes and palms flat on the ground. (For an easier alternative, bend your elbows so that your forearms rest on the ground.) Your body should form a straight line from shoulders to ankles. Hold the pose, engaging your core by sucking in your belly button toward your spine.

Cycle 2:

5. *Sky Reach (15 reps per side)*

Sit on the ground with your legs crossed under you, back upright with good posture. Bring your hands together in front of you and lightly press your fingertips together. Raise your right hand above your head while contracting your left obliques. Return to to the starting position, then raise your left hand above your head while contracting your right obliques. Repeat each move quickly, alternating sides.

6. Chest Clap (30 reps)

Sit on the ground with your legs crossed under you, back upright with good posture. Bring your hands together in front of you and lightly press your fingertips together. Slowly stretch your arms out to the side until they are slightly behind you, then stop and hold the pose for one second. Then bring your arms forward to the starting position, and continue repeating the wide clapping motion in slow, smooth strokes.

7.   *Squat Pulse (30 reps)*

Stand tall with your feet shoulder-width apart and palms pressed together in front of you. Squat down until your knees are at 90-degree angles and hold the position, keeping your abs contracted, for three seconds. Come back to starting position by pushing your weight through your heels. Repeat quickly.

8.   *Buddha Squat (60 seconds)*

Stand tall with your feet shoulder-width apart and palms pressed together in front of you. Squat down until your knees are at 90-degree angles and hold the position, keeping your abs contracted, for 60 seconds.

Cooldown:

After a workout it's important to keep moving the body so that you prevent injuries and soreness as well as increase flexibility and core strength. I recommend taking a few minutes to move your body around. Walk in place, jog gently, circle your arms, lift and lower your shoulders, lift and lower your knees, or dance around. Any sort of movement will do.

For more routines—including 12 weeks of complete workouts, plus 4 weeks of beginners' workouts—check out my training club at jorgecruise.com.

How Much Movement Is Too Much?

We've now been reading and watching headlines about the obesity epidemic and society's tendency toward slothfulness for more than a decade and a half, so it isn't often that the subject of "too much" exercise makes the news. Current government recommendations for exercise ranges from a minimum of 30 minutes of moderate activity five days a week to 15 minutes of vigorous exercise five days a week to an hour of moderate activity every day.

Generally speaking, though, all experts tend to agree that more is usually better—to a point. Remember that rest is an essential part of an exercise routine. If you do not allow your muscles to recover, they won't have time to rebuild, and you also run the risk of overexertion or injury. Make sure you have at least two rest days a week. This is why in some of my routines I recommend that you do strenuous activity on nonconsecutive days; the days in between are your rest days.

Also know that there is a tipping point where exercise can become more harmful than helpful. Although this isn't something most of us will run into, I have seen it happen. A small minority of exercisers may get a bit obsessed with their exercise regimens. Warning signs for extreme exercisers include having a lifestyle that is completely organized around exercise—family, work, and any free time is entirely dedicated to exercise. If you previously suffered from an eating disorder such as anorexia or bulimia, you are at a somewhat higher risk for having an exercise addiction. Check in with friends, family, and your doctor to get a reality check.

You might be overdoing it with your workouts if you hardly ever take a rest day, and find yourself obsessing about the calories you won't be burning, or the weight you might gain, if you do. Other signs that you might need a rest day or shorter sessions are experiencing overuse injuries such as tennis elbow or Achilles injury (and you keep on running), or if you miss important engagements such as a business meeting, the birth of a child, or your wedding.

Your Rx:
Everyday Moving

"Move your body, move your mind."

—Unknown

What can you do specifically to benefit from movement?

Do it.

No kidding around here. That's truly the biggest hurdle for most of us; getting started is the hardest part. However, once you do get your motor going, your body will learn to love it, and pretty soon you won't want to go without it. It's time to take the challenge. Here's how to incorporate regular movement into your life.

Think back now to your personal motivations—remember why you want to move. I want you to commit to doing a moving activity you like three to four times a week. Pick something that fits your life or something that has worked for you in the past. Find a cue and reward for your chosen activity so that you can create habit loops.

Set reminders for yourself to decrease the amount of sitting you do and increase your NEAT. With the formal exercise routines I've shared with you, as well as your nonexercise activities, you'll get all the movement you need.

Now I want you to grab a piece of paper and write the following, then sign and date it, and hang it on your fridge or bedroom wall:

Hardwiring Movement Contract

I, _____ (name), commit to using

_____ , _____ , and _____ as my

cues to trigger my movement habit. I will do

_____ for my movement routine at

least three times a week, and each time I complete

my movement routine I will give myself the following

reward_____ .

Know that your commitment to movement is a preventative measure. It will keep your neurotransmitters elevated, improve your physical health, and create an automatic self-rewarding habit that will add years to your life.

When you are feeling extra stressed and overwhelmed—make double the time to move. Not only will you get double back for every minute you spend exercising, you'll tap into your body and brain's natural relaxation response. And don't forget Choice 1 and Choice 2—Be Imperfectly You and Don't Hold Your Breath—they go perfectly with your moving to balance you out and keep you on track to your best life ever.

How to Start: Your 4-Week Practice

Don't know where to begin with Moving to Improve? Consider doing the following for the next four weeks.

Week 1: Fill out the contract and go on 30-minute walk on three nonconsecutive days this week. Think of a cue and a reward that would appeal to you and help you create your new habit loop.

Week 2: Monitor the steps you take this week using a pedometer or fitness app. Make a goal of 5,000 steps per day. Continue to go on 30-minute walks on three nonconsecutive days this week.

Week 3: Think of fun ways to increase your NEAT and decrease how often you sit! Set an alarm on your phone to go off every hour to remind you to get up and stand or go for a short walk. Continue to monitor the steps, with a goal of 10,000 steps per day, and go on 30-minute walks on three nonconsecutive days this week.

Week 4: Pick your favorite activity from the beginning of this chapter and begin implementing the weekly schedule into your routine. Spend a day preparing: buy any accessories you need, find out workout class schedules or workout buddies, and think of a cue and a reward to create your new habit loop. (After you complete your first activity schedule, be sure to pick another movement that you'd like to try!)

Congratulations! You now know the three choices. You have all the knowledge you need to start over at any given moment of any day. With the three choices, you can take control of your life.

AFTERWORD
Standing in the Sun

"It's better to be alone than in the wrong relationship. Never settle for anything less than what you want and desire."

— Rick Ayers, Sam's dad and my father-in-law

After you truly discover and choose to be who you are at your core, it is the most freeing thing you could ever feel. I am so proud to say to myself every day, "I LOVE ME." I have never felt more intelligent and confident about who I am as a husband, father, brother, son, author, trainer, and dancer. But the important point of my story here is that once you choose to love yourself, life gets pretty amazing. So you might as well start doing it before life fast-forwards and, before you know it, your gray-haired self is watching your kids grow up in seconds. Trust me—I'm the one who waited 39 years to choose to accept my identity. It's been seven years now since I've come out as a gay man, and since then my life has been truly blessed.

My mastering of the three choices brought me, finally, to a place where I knew exactly who I was as a person and loved myself for who I was. I knew what I wanted out of life by knowing who I truly was. I am someone who cherishes relationships, needs calm in my life, and loves the comfort of family and friends. Because I identified who I was at my core, I never have to settle in any aspect of my life, whether it's career, health, relationships—you name it.

Ultimately the three choices are all about loving yourself. Be Imperfectly You, Don't Hold Your Breath, Move to Improve . . . each is a simple act of self-love. Each time you give yourself the time and energy to make one of these choices, you are standing in the sun saying to yourself, *I am deserving.* And you are! You deserve your own love and support, to make yourself a priority, to feel good, to have what you want *and* what you really want. You deserve all the love you desire from others. You deserve everything.

Now, I can't promise you will find your soul mate. (I am not in control of anyone's journey or path.) But I can tell you the path that led me to mine.

And it can be all summed up in two simple words . . .

Never Settle

After my divorce, I felt intimidated at the thought of dating. I didn't have a "little black book" saved from before I met my wife. Sure, I'd had a few relationships in my young adulthood with women, but never with a man. This was a whole new "workout" for me to learn, so to say. However, with the help of the three choices, I came to understand that I'm someone who cherishes connection. So, while I was in no rush, I knew that I would want to find love again when the time was right.

But, boy, did dating change over those last 20 years! From swiping right on a dating app to having to learn the hard way that you can never assume you're monogamous, I definitely had my ups and downs. But I was determined to keep going, to live into the three choices, to not to settle for anything less than what I deserved and wanted in *every* area of my life.

After kissing a few frogs, going through a little heartbreak, and making a few mistakes, I decided to take a breather and just focus on doing what brought me joy in the present. I wasn't worried about finding "the One" because I was finally in a place where I loved myself. After all those frogs, I finally knew what I was looking for and wasn't going to settle for a subpar relationship, just for the sake of being in one.

I'll tell you what the choices that led me to a blessed life were: I chose to stop dating and to only do the things that provided me with happiness, such as spending time with my kids, reading in my favorite lounge chair, sleeping in when I could, taking trips with friends to Cabo just because, watching movies I've always wanted to watch—like the entire Harry Potter series in four days—and exploring the city I've always lived in.

About a year into my dating breather, I was in Los Angeles filming an exercise segment for *Extra*. After filming I had some free time, and when my best friend Leslie asked me to be her wingman for a blind date she was iffy about, I agreed. (Just in case you didn't know, gay men are the best wingmen!) So, off we went to a hip West Hollywood spot called The Church Key on Sunset Boulevard.

The place wasn't really my scene. In fact, seven years ago, before everything had changed, I would have felt completely out of place and self-consciously inched my way to the door. Now, however, I felt oddly at home because I was at home on the inside, no matter what was happening on the outside. I loved myself—*all of myself.*

Anyway, as Leslie chatted with her date, I was casually just hanging out when I saw a stunning blond nearby. Totally intrigued, I went over and struck up a conversation with the person I would come to know as Sam. As the night wore on, we talked about everything under the sun, from our childhoods to our mutual interest in fitness to our love for Beyoncé . . . And I shared the real me. In fact, thanks to the advice of my amazing friend and fellow author Steve Harvey, I straight up told him very early in our conversation that I had two kids I was very committed to and was looking for a serious relationship. Sam didn't bat an eyelash, unlike the others before him.

When it was time to say good-bye, we exchanged numbers and started texting right away. Then came our long phone calls and marathon FaceTimes—and a $400 phone bill from roaming charges while I was on a Disney cruise the following week with my sons! After I returned, we saw each other as soon as we could, and things just grew from there. I proposed about a year later, and we were married July 2, 2016 (aka the best day of my entire life!).

Sam and I have the kind of relationship that I'd always dreamed about but wasn't totally sure was possible. He brings the calm to my Latin fire, but most important, we complement each other in a way that only a yin yang could represent. Since we've met, we have both grown and evolved to what I consider the best versions of ourselves. He helps me, and I help him. We are always on the same team. And I couldn't imagine a day without him.

Life has a funny way of giving you exactly what you want or something even better, once you stop settling and know you deserve it.

Live the Life You *Really* Want

Seven years ago, I felt like my life was falling apart and wouldn't ever fall back together. Yet, choice by choice and day by day, every-thing did come together into a life beyond my wildest dreams. There were a few big crossroads along the way, but what made the most impact were my everyday choices. In particular, the more I made these three choices, the more I was able to experience and create everything I really, *really* wanted. With each passing day, I loved myself a little more; got clearer on what I wanted and needed for real, lasting happiness; and knew that I deserved nothing less. I was finally standing in the sun.

That is what I want for you. I want you to experience the inner peace that comes when you totally love yourself, to know that you are deserving just as you are, and to have the confidence to move toward your desires. I want you to have what you *really* want.

Make these three choices on a consistent basis. Do only the things that feel like freedom to you, and happiness will follow. Remember to have fun. Spend time with your family and friends. Read more. Create something you're proud of. Make your own rules and then break them. Take trips alone. Discover your hidden talents.

Flaunt your flaws. Love yourself. Be selfish without being malevolent. Treat yourself just because you deserve it.

You deserve to stand in the sun; you deserve it all.

BIBLIOGRAPHY

How to Begin: Break Your Illusions

Najjar, Lubna. "The Power of Choice." *The Huffington Post*, April 16, 2015. http://www.huffingtonpost.com/lubna-najjar/the-power-of-choice_1_b _6683212.html.

"Number of Pages Book Readers Read before They Abandon a Book 2013 | Survey." Statista, 2013. http://www.statista.com/statistics/261933 /number-of-pages-book-readersread-before-they-abandon-a-book.

Rhomberg, Andrew. "If You Sell the Book, Will They Read It?" Digital Book World, September 16, 2015. http://www.digitalbookworld.com/2015 /if-you-sell-the-book-will-they-read-it.

"Wheel of Emotions (Worksheet) | Therapist Aid." TherapistAid.com, 2015. http://www.therapistaid.com/therapy-worksheet/wheel-of-emotions.

Choice 1: Be Imperfectly You

Alexander, Ronald. "5 Steps to Make Affirmations Work for You." *Psychology Today*, August 15, 2011. http://www.psychologytoday.com/blog/the-wise -open-mind/201108/5-steps-make-affirmations-work-you.

Begley, Sharon. "Rewiring Your Emotions." *Mindful*, July 27, 2013. http://www .mindful.org/rewiring-your-emotions.

Brafman, Rom. "Don't Be Swayed." *Psychology Today*, August 18, 2008. http://www.psychologytoday.com/blog/dont-be-swayed.

Bryan, J., Z. Baker, and R. Tou. "Prevent the Blue, Be True to You: Authenticity Buffers the Negative Impact of Loneliness on Alcohol-Related Problems, Physical Symptoms, and Depressive and Anxiety Symptoms." *Journal of Health Psychology*, October 2015. DOI:10.1177/1359105315609090.

Colier, Nancy. "Why Our Thoughts Are Not Real." *Psychology Today*, August 23, 2013. http://www.psychologytoday.com/blog/inviting-monkey-tea /201308/why-our-thoughts-are-not-real.

Creswell, J.D., J.M. Dutcher, W.M.P. Klein, P.R. Harris, and J.M. Levine. "Self-Affirmation Improves Problem-Solving under Stress." *PLOS ONE* 8, 5 (2013): e62593. DOI:10.1371/journal.pone.0062593.

Dispenza, Joe. "Evolve Your Brain: The Science of Changing Your Mind (Part 1)." *Pathways to Family Wellness* 15 (2007). http://pathwaystofamily wellness.org/Inspirational/evolve-your-brianthe-science-of-changing -your-mind-part-1.html.

— — —. "Evolve Your Brain." Dr Joe Dispenza. http://www.drjoedispenza.com /index.php?page_id=Evolve-Your-Brain.

"Don't Believe Everything You Think." Cleveland Clinic, 2012. http://www .clevelandclinicwellness.com/programs/NewSFN/pages/default.aspx ?Lesson=3&Topic=2&UserId=00000000-0000-0000-0000 -000000000705.

Fabrega, Marelisa. "119 Journal Prompts for Your Journal Jar." Daring to Live Fully, September 17, 2016. http://www.daringtolivefully.com /journal-prompts.

Hamilton, David R. "Does Your Brain Distinguish Real from Imaginary?" David R Hamilton PhD: Using Science to Inspire, October 31, 2014. http://www .drdavidhamilton.com/does-yourbrain-distinguish-real-from-imaginary.

Handel, Steven. "The Science of Self-Affirmations." The Emotion Machine, May 8, 2013. http://www.theemotionmachine.com/the-science-of-self -affirmations.

Heppner, W., M. Kernis, J. Nezlek, J. Foster, C. Lakey, and B. Goldman. "Within-Person Relationships among Daily Self-Esteem, Need Satisfaction, and Authenticity." *Psychological Science* 19, 11 (2008): 1140-45. DOI:10.1111/j.1467-9280.2008.02215.x.

Holmes, Lindsay. "Self-Affirmations Can Boost Performance, Study Shows." *The Huffington Post*, May 14, 2015. http://www.huffingtonpost.com /2015/04/16/self-affirmations-boost-performance_n_7079350.html.

Katie, Byron. "Do the Work." The Work. Byron Katie International, Inc., September 6, 2015. http://www.thework.com/en/do-work.

Khoshaba, Deborah, Psy.D. "How We Story Our Life Experience Matters." *Psychology Today*, March 19, 2014. http://www.psychologytoday.com /blog/get-hardy/201403/how-we-story-our-life-experience-matters.

Liou, Stephanie. "Neuroplasticity." HOPES: Huntington's Outreach Project for Education at Stanford, June 26, 2010. http://web.stanford.edu/group /hopes/cgi-bin/hopes_test/neuroplasticity.

McGraw, Phillip C., Dr. "Defining Your Authentic Self | Dr. Phil." Dr Phil, July 13, 2005. http://www.drphil.com/advice/defining-your-authenticself.

Murray, Bridget. "Writing to Heal." *Monitor on Psychology* 33, 6 (June 2002): 54. http://www.apa.org/monitor/jun02/writing.aspx.

Nguyen, Thai. "10 Surprising Benefits You'll Get from Keeping a Journal." *The Huffington Post*, April 15, 2015. http://www.huffingtonpost.com/thai -nguyen/benefits-of-journaling-_b_6648884.html.

Pascual-Leone, A., D. Nguyet, L.G. Cohen, Brasil-Neto, A. Cammarota, and M. Hallett. "Modulation of Muscle Responses Evoked by Transcranial Magnetic Stimulation During the Acquisition of New Fine Motor Skills." *Journal of Neurophysiology* 74, 3 (September 1995): 1037–45. PMID:7500130.

Purcell, Maud. "The Health Benefits of Journaling | Psych Central." *Psych Central*, May 17, 2016. http://www.psychcentral.com/lib/the-health-benefits -of-journaling.

Schmeichel, B.J., and K. Vohs. "Self-Affirmation and Self-Control: Affirming Core Values Counteracts Ego Depletion." *Journal of Personality and Social Psychology* 96, 4 (April 2009):770-82. DOI:10.1037/a0014635.

Stinson, D.A., C. Logel, S. Shepherd, and M.P. Zanna. "Rewriting the Self-Fulfilling Prophecy of Social Rejection: Self-Affirmation Improves Relational Security and Social Behavior up to 2 Months Later." *Psychological Science* 22, 9 (2011):1145-49. DOI:10.1177/0956797611417725.

Wright, Karen. "Dare to Be Yourself." *Psychology Today*, May 1, 2008. http:// www.psychologytoday.com/articles/200805/dare-be-yourself.

Choice 2: Don't Hold Your Breath

"Benefits of Physical Activity." National Heart, Lung, and Blood Institute, June 22, 2016. https://www.nhlbi.nih.gov/health/health-topics/topics /phys/benefits.

Bhasin, M., et al. "Relaxation Response Induces Temporal Transcriptome Changes in Energy Metabolism, Insulin Secretion and Inflammatory Pathways." *PLOS ONE* 8, 5 (2013): e62817. DOI:10.1371/journal .pone.0062817.

"Breathe Deeply to Activate Vagus Nerve." Travel and Health. Accessed January 6, 2016. https://sites.google.com/site/stanleyguansite/health /health-tips/breathe-deeply-to-activate-vagus-nerve.

"Breathing Exercises," American Lung Association. Accessed January 6, 2016. http://www.lung.org/lung-health-and-diseases/protecting -your-lungs/breathing-exercises.html.

Brown, R., and P. Gerbarg. "Sudarshan Kriya Yogic Breathing in the Treatment of Stress, Anxiety, and Depression: Part I—Neurophysiologic Model." *The Journal of Alternative and Complementary Medicine* 11, 1 (March 2005): 189–201. DOI:10.1089/acm.2005.11.189.

Brown, R., and P. Gerbarg. "Yoga Breathing, Meditation, and Longevity." *Annals of the New York Academy of Sciences* 1172, 1 (2009): 54–62. DOI:10.1111/j.1749-6632.2009.04394.x.

Carpenter, Siri. "Your Guide to a Healthy, Happy Tummy." *Prevention*, November 3, 2011. Accessed January 6, 2016. http://www.prevention .com/health/health-concerns/solutions-stomach-pain-heartburn-and -digestion-problems.

Chien, H., Y. Chung, M. Yeh, and J. Lee. "Breathing Exercise Combined with Cognitive Behavioural Intervention Improves Sleep Quality and Heart Rate Variability in Major Depression." *Journal of Clinical Nursing* 24, 21–22 (2015): 3206–14. DOI:10.1111/jocn.12972.

Collins, C. "Yoga: Intuition, Preventive Medicine, and Treatment." *Journal of Obstetric, Gynecologic, & Neonatal Nursing* 27, 5 (1998): 563–68. PMID:9773368.

"Coping with Multiple Sclerosis," Multiple Sclerosis Foundation. Accessed January 6, 2016. http://msfocus.org/article-details.aspx?articleID=12.

Eherer, A., et al. "Positive Effect of Abdominal Breathing Exercise on Gastro-esophageal Reflux Disease: A Randomized, Controlled Study." *The American Journal of Gastroenterology* 107, 3 (2011): 372–78. DOI:10.1038/ ajg.2011.420.

Gallego, J., E. Nsegbe, and E. Durand. "Learning in Respiratory Control." *Behavior Modification* 25, 4 (2001): 495–512. PMID:11530713.

Grossman, E., A. Grossman, M. Schein, R. Zimlichman, and B. Gavish. "Breathing-Control Lowers Blood Pressure." *Journal of Human Hypertension* 15, 4 (2001): 263–69. DOI:10.1038/sj.jhh.1001147.

Guz, A. "Brain, Breathing and Breathlessness." *Respiration Physiology* 109, 3 (1997): 197–204. PMID:9342797.

Hanna, Raven. "Science Notes 2005: This Is Your Brain on Meditation." *Science Notes*, 2005. Accessed January 6, 2016. http://sciencenotes.ucsc .edu/0501/meditate/index.html.

Hoge, E., et al. "Loving-Kindness Meditation Practice Associated with Longer Telomeres in Women." *Brain, Behavior, and Immunity* 32 (2013): 159–63. DOI:10.1016/j.bbi.2013.04.005.

Jerath, R., J. Edry, V. Barnes, and V. Jerath. "Physiology of Long Pranayamic Breathing: Neural Respiratory Elements May Provide a Mechanism that Explains How Slow Deep Breathing Shifts the Autonomic Nervous System." *Medical Hypotheses* 67, 3 (2006): 566–71. DOI:10.1016/j.mehy .2006.02.042.

Kox, M., L. Eijk, J. Zwaag, J. Wildenberg, F. Sweep, J. Hoeven, and P. Pickkers. "Voluntary Activation of the Sympathetic Nervous System and Attenuation of the Innate Immune Response in Humans." *Proceedings of the National Academy of Sciences* 111, 20 (2014): 7379–84. DOI:10.1073 /pnas.1322174111.

Lejuwaan, Jordan. "The Wim Hof Method *Revealed* — How to Consciously Control Your Immune System." HighExistence. Accessed January 6, 2016. http://highexistence.com/the-wim-hof-method-revealed-how-to -consciously-control-your-immune-system.

"Lungs, Lungs Information, Breathing Facts, News, Photos — National Geographic." National Geographic. Accessed January 6, 2016. http://science .nationalgeographic.com/science/health-and-human-body/human-body /lungs-article.

Martarelli, D., M. Cocchioni, S. Scuri, and P. Pompei. "Diaphragmatic Breathing Reduces Exercise-Induced Oxidative Stress." *Evidence-Based Complementary and Alternative Medicine* (2011): 1–10. DOI:10.1093/ecam /nep169.

Mayo Clinic Staff. "Stress Management." Mayo Clinic, May 8, 2014. Accessed January 6, 2016. http://www.mayoclinic.org/healthy-lifestyle/stress -management/in-depth/relaxation-technique/art-20045368.

"The Mental Health Benefits of Deep Breathing." Accessed January 6, 2016. http://www.notacoward.com/blog/the-mental-health-benefits-of-deep -breathing.

Neupert, Geoff. "The Most Important Exercise Missing from Your Workout." *Men's Health*, October 29, 2014. http://www.menshealth.com/fitness /diaphragmatic-breathing.

Pavlov, V., and K. Tracey. "The Cholinergic Anti-Inflammatory Pathway." *Brain, Behavior, and Immunity* 19, 6 (December 2005): 493–99. DOI:10.1016 /j.bbi.2005.03.015.

Schultz, Colin. "Breathing Deeply May Actually Boost Your Body's Immune System," *Smithsonian Magazine*. Accessed January 6, 2016. http://www .smithsonianmag.com/smart-news/breathing-deeply-may-actually-boost -your-bodys-immune-system-180951361/?no-ist.

Seppälä, E., et al. "Breathing-Based Meditation Decreases Posttraumat- ic Stress Disorder Symptoms in U.S. Military Veterans: A Randomized Controlled Longitudinal Study." *Journal of Traumatic Stress* 27, 4 (2014): 397–405. DOI:10.1002/jts.21936.

Shaw, B., and I. Shaw. "Pulmonary Function and Abdominal and Thoracic Kinematic Changes Following Aerobic and Inspiratory Resistive Diaphrag- matic Breathing Training in Asthmatics." *Lung* 189, 2 (2011): 131–39. DOI:10.1007/s00408-011-9281-8.

Shaw, I., B. Shaw, and G. Brown. "Role of Diaphragmatic Breathing and Aerobic Exercise in Improving Pulmonary Function and Maximal Oxygen Consumption in Asthmatics." *Science & Sports* 25, 3 (2010): 139–45. DOI:10.1016/j.scispo.2009.10.003.

Sovik, R. "The Science of Breathing—the Yogic View." In E. A. Mayer and C. B. Saper, eds., *Progress in Brain Research, Vol 122: The Biological Basis for Mind Body Interactions*. New York: Elsevier Science BV, 2000: 491–505.

Williams, Matthew. "Take a Deep Breath: The Physiology of Slow Deep Breath- ing." Mindfulness, MD, June 27, 2015. Accessed January 6, 2016. http:// www.mindfulnessmd.com/2015/06/27/neuroscience-of-mindfulness-take -a-deep-breath.

Choice 3: Move to Improve

Berardi, John. "The Elephant in Your Brain." Idea Health & Fitness Association, October 1, 2014. Accessed January 6, 2016. http://www.ideafit.com /fitness-library/the-elephant-in-your-brain.

Blumenthal, J., et al. "Effects of Exercise Training on Older Patients with Major Depression." *Archives of Internal Medicine* 159, 19 (1999). DOI:10.1001/ archinte.159.19.2349.

Brené, S., A. Bjørnebekk, E. Åberg, A. Mathé, L. Olson, and M. Werme. "Running Is Rewarding and Antidepressive." *Physiology & Behavior* 92, 1–2 (2007): 136–40. DOI:10.1016/j.physbeh.2007.05.015.

Buckley, J., J. Cohen, A. Kramer, E. Mcauley, and S. Mullen. "Cognitive Control in the Self-Regulation of Physical Activity and Sedentary Behavior." *Frontiers in Human Neuroscience* 8 (2014). DOI:10.3389/fnhum.2014 .00747.

Cohen, E., R. Ejsmond-Frey, N. Knight, and R. Dunbar. "Rowers' High: Behavioural Synchrony Is Correlated with Elevated Pain Thresholds." *Biology Letters* 6, 1 (2009): 106–08. DOI:10.1098/rsbl.2009.0670.

Cooney, G., K. Dwan, and G. Mead. "Exercise for Depression." *JAMA Internal Medicine* 311, 23 (2014): 2432–33. DOI:10.1001/jama.2014.4930.

Cuddy, Amy. "Your Body Language Shapes Who You Are." TED. June 2012, Accessed January 6, 2016. https://www.ted.com/talks/amy_cuddy _your_body_language_shapes_who_you_are.

Duhigg, Charles. "The Power of Habit: Charles Duhigg at TEDxTeachersCollege." August 18, 2013, Accessed January 6, 2016. https://www.youtube .com/watch?v=OMbsGBlpP30.

———. *The Power of Habit: Why We Do What We Do in Life and Business*. New York: Random House, 2012.

Erickson, K., et al. "Exercise Training Increases Size of Hippocampus and Improves Memory." *Proceedings of the National Academy of Sciences* 108, 7 (2011): 3017–22. DOI:10.1073/pnas.1015950108.

Erickson, K., D. Miller, and K. Roecklein. "The Aging Hippocampus: Interactions between Exercise, Depression, and BDNF." *The Neuroscientist* 18, 1 (2011): 82–97. DOI:10.1177/1073858410397054.

Erickson, K., R. Leckie, and A. Weinstein. "Physical Activity, Fitness, and Gray Matter Volume." *Neurobiology of Aging* 35 (2014). DOI:0.1016/j.neurobiolaging.2014.03.034.

Farina, N., J. Rusted, and N. Tabet. "The Effect of Exercise Interventions on Cognitive Outcome in Alzheimer's Disease: A Systematic Review." *International Psychogeriatrics* (2013): 1–10. DOI:10.1017/S1041610213001385.

Fuqua, J., and A. Rogol. "Neuroendocrine Alterations in the Exercising Human: Implications for Energy Homeostasis." *Metabolism* 62, 7 (2013): 911–21. DOI:10.1016/j.metabol.2013.01.016.

Godman, Heidi. "Regular Exercise Changes the Brain to Improve Memory, Thinking Skills." Harvard Health Publications, November 29, 2016. http://www.health.harvard.edu/blog/regular-exercise-changes-brain-improve-memory-thinking-skills-201404097110.

Gomez-Pinilla, F., and C. Hillman. "The Influence of Exercise on Cognitive Abilities." *Comprehensive Physiology* 3, 1 (2013): 403–28. DOI:10.1002/cphy.c110063.

Guiney, H., and L. Machado. "Benefits of Regular Aerobic Exercise for Executive Functioning in Healthy Populations." *Psychonomic Bulletin & Review* 20, 1 (2013): 73–86. DOI:10.3758/s13423-012-0345-4.

Hegberg, N., and E. Tone. "Physical Activity and Stress Resilience: Considering Those At-Risk for Developing Mental Health Problems." *Mental Health and Physical Activity* 8 (2015): 1–7. DOI:10.1016/j.mhpa.2014.10.001.

Josefsson, T., M. Lindwall, and T. Archer. "Physical Exercise Intervention in Depressive Disorders: Meta-analysis and Systematic Review." *Scandinavian Journal of Medicine & Science in Sports* 24, 2 (2013): 259–72. DOI:10.1111/sms.12050.

Kamp, C., B. Sperlich, and H. Holmberg. "Exercise Reduces the Symptoms of Attention-Deficit/Hyperactivity Disorder and Improves Social Behaviour, Motor Skills, Strength and Neuropsychological Parameters." *Acta Paediatrica* 103, 7 (2014): 709–14. DOI:10.1111/apa.12628.

Levine, J. "Non-Exercise Activity Thermogenesis (NEAT)." *Nutrition Reviews* 62, 2 (2004): S82–S97. DOI:10.1111/j.1753-4887.2004.tb00094.x.

Mcewen, B. "Stress and the Individual." *Archives of Internal Medicine* 153, 18 (1993): 2093–101. PMID:8379800.

Mura, G., M. Moro, S. Patten, and M. Carta. "Exercise as an Add-On Strategy for the Treatment of Major Depressive Disorder: A Systematic Review." *CNS Spectrums* 19, 6 (2014): 496–508. DOI:10.1017/S1092852913000953.

Nelson, Nicole. "Allostasis: A New View of Stress and How It Affects the Body." *Massage Today*, July 2013. Accessed January 6, 2016. http://www.massagetoday.com/mpacms/mt/article.php?id=14783.

Penedo, F., and J. Dahn. "Exercise and Well-Being: A Review of Mental and Physical Health Benefits Associated with Physical Activity." *Current Opinion in Psychiatry* 18, 2 (2005): 189–93. PMID:16639173.

Phillips, C., M. Baktir, M. Srivatsan, and A. Salehi. "Neuroprotective Effects of Physical Activity on the Brain: A Closer Look at Trophic Factor Signaling." *Frontiers in Cellular Neuroscience* 8 (2014): 170. DOI: 10.3389/fncel.2014.00170.

Raichlen, D., A. Foster, G. Gerdeman, A. Seillier, and A. Giuffrida. "Wired to Run: Exercise-Induced Endocannabinoid Signaling in Humans and Cursorial Mammals with Implications for the 'Runner's High.'" *Journal of Experimental Biology* 215, 8 (2012): 1331–36. DOI:10.1242/jeb.063677.

"Rated Perceived Exertion (RPE) Scale." Cleveland Clinic. Accessed January 6, 2016. http://my.clevelandclinic.org/services/heart/prevention/exercise/rpe-scale.

Rosenbaum, S., A. Tiedemann, C. Sherrington, J. Curtis, and P. Ward. "Physical Activity Interventions for People with Mental Illness." *The Journal of Clinical Psychiatry* 75, 9 (2014): 964–974. DOI:10.4088/JCP.13r08765.

Ruscheweyh, R., et al. "Physical Activity and Memory Functions: An Interventional Study." *Neurobiology of Aging* 32, 7 (2011): 1304–19. DOI:10.1016/j.neurobiolaging.2009.08.001.

Stathopoulou, G., M. Powers, A. Berry, J. Smits, and M. Otto. "Exercise Interventions for Mental Health: A Qutative and Qualitative Review." *Clinical Psychology: Science and Practice* 13, 2 (2006): 179–93. DOI:10.1111/j.1468-2850.2006.00021.x.

Ströhle, A., C. Feller, M. Onken, F. Godemann, A. Heinz, and F. Dimeo. "The Acute Antipanic Activity of Aerobic Exercise." *American Journal of Psychiatry* 162, 12 (2005): 2376–78. DOI:10.1176/appi.ajp.162.12.2376.

Swardfager, W., et al. "Cardiopulmonary Fitness Is Associated with Cognitive Performance in Patients with Coronary Artery Disease." *Journal of the American Geriatrics Society* 58, 8 (2010): 1519–25. DOI:10.1111/j.1532-5415.2010.02966.x.

Szuhany, K., M. Bugatti, and M. Otto. "A Meta-Analytic Review of the Effects of Exercise on Brain-Derived Neurotrophic Factor." *Journal of Psychiatric Research* 60 (2015): 56–64. DOI:10.1016/j.jpsychires.2014.10.003.

Tantimonaco, M., R. Ceci, S. Sabatini, M. Catani, A. Rossi, V. Gasperi, and M. Maccarrone. "Physical Activity and the Endocannabinoid System: An Overview." *Cellular and Molecular Life Sciences* 71, 14 (2014): 2681–98. DOI:10.1007/s00018-014-1575-6.

Tarumi, T., and R. Zhang. "Cerebral Hemodynamics of the Aging Brain: Risk of Alzheimer Disease and Benefit of Aerobic Exercise. *Frontiers in Physiology* 5 (2014). DOI:10.3389/fphys.2014.00006.

Weir, Kirsten. "The Exercise Effect." *Monitor on Psychology* 42, 11 (December 2011): 48. http://www.apa.org/monitor/2011/12/exercise.aspx.

Zschucke, E., K. Gaudlitz, K., and A. Ströhle. "Exercise and Physical Activity in Mental Disorders: Clinical and Experimental Evidence." *Journal of Preventive Medicine & Public Health* 46, 1 (2013). DOI:10.3961/jpmph .2013.46.S.S12.

ACKNOWLEDGMENTS

I owe a tremendous amount of gratitude to my editor Patricia Gift. Without your incredible patience and direction, *The 3 Choices* would have never come to life. Thank you for your overwhelming love and support for this material; you are, without exception, the most talented editor I have ever worked with.

A huge thanks to my dear friend and publisher Reid Tracy, without whom this book would have never come to fruition. Working with you has been the most exceptional experience of my entire career. Thank you for pushing me to write this book and giving me the confidence to tell my story.

To Louise Hay, thank you for being my biggest role model and supporter since I was 25 years old. Without your mentorship and support, I would not be the man that I am today. Thank you for challenging me to transform my thinking and live in my authentic life.

I want to thank Richelle Zizian Fredson for your limitless talent and help in bringing *The 3 Choices* and its message to the world. Thank you to the supreme team at Hay House: Anne Barthel, Nicolette Salamanca Young, Lindsay McGinty, Diane Thomas, Nick C. Welch, and Tricia Breidenthal.

A very special thank-you to my husband, Sam, for being a constant source of calm, support, love, and encouragement in my life. You are the fuel to my fire, and I love you so much.

To my children, Parker and Owen, thank you for inspiring me to write this book. Every lesson in here was written for you to grow from. Thank you for your endless love and support, I love you both very much. I thank my sister, Marta, for being my rock and lifting me up when I need it most. Thanks to my beautiful family, Mel,

Joan, Rick, Kurt, Blaze, and Gigi, for being so supportive; and to my mother, Gloria, who is my brilliant star in the sky. I am so grateful to my co-parent and friend, Heather, for being my everything during the first chapter of my life; I cherish our friendship and the family we have made together.

I'd also like to thank my friends and supporters: Don Miguel Ruiz, Steve Harvey, Marjorie Harvey, Broderick Harvey Jr., Gerald Washington, Meagan Dotson, Thabiti Stephens, Anthony Robbins, Oprah Winfrey, Cristina Saralegui, former president Bill Clinton, Dr. Mehmet Oz, James Avenell, Carol Brooks, Maggie Jacqua, Mary Ellen Keating, Alisa Schnaars, Lashaun Dale, Raymond Garcia, Cris Abrego, Flavio Morales, Jairek Robbins, Don Miguel Ruiz, Gabrielle Bernstein, Jeff Williams, Jay Blank, Julz Arney, Andreas Koch, Lisa Gregorisch-Dempsey, Mario Lopez, Lauren Hennessy, Leslie Marcus, Khloe Kardashian, John Redman, Jessica Marlow, Lili Estefan, Chris Park, Dr. David Katz, Mark Sisson, Bob Wietrak, Dr. Darren Farnesi, Danielle Schaffer, Dr. Robert Schaffer, Brooke Burke, Alex Duda, Patty Neger, Dr. Travis Stork, Dr. Jen Berman, Marco Borges, Richard Galanti, Barrie Galanti, Dr. Tess Mauricio, Pennie Clark Ianniciello, Terence Noonan, Natalie Bubnis, Scott Eason, Lisa Wheeler, Larissa Matson, Amy Cohn, Erica Merrell, Marissa McCormick, Maha Tahiri, Dr. Andrew Weil, Jennifer Wilson, Janet Annino, Dr. Christiane Northrup, David Jackson, Jacqui Stafford, and Amanda Molina.

ABOUT THE AUTHOR

JORGE CRUISE, internationally recognized #1 *New York Times* best-selling author and wellness coach, had a very difficult start to life. He was raised by his grandmother with oppressive rules and struggled with weight—life was a struggle. Jorge overcame the odds and is now recognized as a leading expert in his field, has found the love of his life, and is living the career of his dreams, with over eight million books sold. Jorge found his epic life. *The 3 Choices* will teach you everything you need to know to live yours.

Connect with Jorge socially at:
Facebook.com/JorgeCruise
YouTube.com/JorgeCruise
Instagram.com/JorgeCruise
Twitter.com/JorgeCruise

Join Jorge's community for updates and news. Stay connected by visiting: JorgeCruise.com.

Hay House Titles of Related Interest

YOU CAN HEAL YOUR LIFE, the movie,
starring Louise Hay & Friends
(available as a 1-DVD program and an expanded 2-DVD set)
Watch the trailer at: www.LouiseHayMovie.com

THE SHIFT, the movie,
starring Dr. Wayne W. Dyer
(available as a 1-DVD program and an expanded 2-DVD set)
Watch the trailer at: www.DyerMovie.com

• • •

E-SQUARED: Nine Do-It-Yourself Energy Experiments That Prove Your Thoughts Create Your Reality, by Pam Grout

LIFE LOVES YOU: 7 Spiritual Practices to Heal Your Life,
by Louise Hay and Robert Holden

MIRACLES NOW: 108 Life-Changing Tools for Less Stress, More Flow, and Finding Your True Purpose, by Gabrielle Bernstein

RESILIENCE FROM THE HEART: The Power to Thrive in Life's Extremes, by Gregg Braden

*WHO WOULD YOU BE WITHOUT YOUR STORY?:
Dialogues with Byron Katie*, by Byron Katie

All of the above are available at your local bookstore,
or may be ordered by contacting Hay House (see next page).

• • •

We hope you enjoyed this Hay House book. If you'd like to receive our online catalog featuring additional information on Hay House books and products, or if you'd like to find out more about the Hay Foundation, please contact:

Hay House, Inc., P.O. Box 5100, Carlsbad, CA 92018-5100
(760) 431-7695 or (800) 654-5126
(760) 431-6948 (fax) or (800) 650-5115 (fax)
www.hayhouse.com® • www.hayfoundation.org

■ ■ ■

Published and distributed in Australia by: Hay House Australia Pty. Ltd., 18/36 Ralph St., Alexandria NSW 2015 • *Phone:* 612-9669-4299 *Fax:* 612-9669-4144 • www.hayhouse.com.au

Published and distributed in the United Kingdom by: Hay House UK, Ltd., Astley House, 33 Notting Hill Gate, London W11 3JQ *Phone:* 44-20-3675-2450 • *Fax:* 44-20-3675-2451 • www.hayhouse.co.uk

Published and distributed in the Republic of South Africa by: Hay House SA (Pty), Ltd., P.O. Box 990, Witkoppen 2068 info@hayhouse.co.za • www.hayhouse.co.za

Published in India by: Hay House Publishers India, Muskaan Complex, Plot No. 3, B-2, Vasant Kunj, New Delhi 110 070 • *Phone:* 91-11-4176-1620 *Fax:* 91-11-4176-1630 • www.hayhouse.co.in

Distributed in Canada by: Raincoast Books, 2440 Viking Way, Richmond, B.C. V6V 1N2 • *Phone:* 1-800-663-5714 • *Fax:* 1-800-565-3770 www.raincoast.com

■ ■ ■

Take Your Soul on a Vacation

Visit www.HealYourLife.com® to regroup, recharge, and reconnect with your own magnificence. Featuring blogs, mind-body-spirit news, and life-changing wisdom from Louise Hay and friends.

Visit www.HealYourLife.com today!